Dr. Gary Goodman's highly successful telephone training seminar has taught thousands of salespeople how to sell by telephone. His method of telemarketing has been used by every major industry in America for more than fourteen years, and his *Telephone Effectiveness Newsletter* has become a recognized sales tool throughout the country. Dr. Goodman, author of the best-selling *Winning by Telephone* (Prentice-Hall), is a consultant to many Fortune 500 corporations as well as a popular convention speaker before national trade and professional associations.

Prentice-Hall International, Inc., *London*
Prentice-Hall of Australia Pty. Limited, *Sydney*
Prentice-Hall Canada Inc., *Toronto*
Prentice-Hall of India Private Limited, *New Delhi*
Prentice-Hall of Japan, Inc., *Tokyo*
Prentice-Hall of Southeast Asia Pte. Ltd., *Singapore*
Whitehall Books Limited, *Wellington, New Zealand*
Editora Prentice-Hall do Brasil Ltda., *Rio de Janeiro*

Dr. Gary S. Goodman

Reach Out & Sell Someone

Phone Your Way to Profit and Success Through the Goodman System of Telemarketing

A SPECTRUM BOOK

Prentice-Hall, Inc., Englewood Cliffs, New Jersey 07632

Library of Congress Cataloging in Publication Data

Goodman, Gary S.
    Reach out and sell someone.

    "A Spectrum Book."
    Includes index
    1. Telephone selling. I. Title. II. Title:
Reach out and sell someone.
HF5438.3.G66 1983   658.8'5   83-2906
ISBN 0-13-753632-1
ISBN 0-13-753624-0 (pbk.)

This book is available at a special discount when ordered
in bulk quantities. Contact Prentice-Hall, Inc., General
Publishing Division, Special Sales, Englewood Cliffs, N.J. 07632

The phrase "Reach Out and Sell Someone" has been used in conjunction
with seminars in telephone marketing offered by the author over the
past several years throughout the United States. Neither the author
nor the publisher is presently affiliated with any telephone company.

2   3   4   5   6   7   8   9   10

ISBN 0-13-753632-1

ISBN 0-13-753624-0 {PBK.}

Editorial/production supervision by Rita Young
Cover design © 1983 by Jeannette Jacobs
Manufacturing buyer: Pat Mahoney

This book is dedicated to my wife, best friend, and colleague, Dr. Deanne Honeyman-Goodman; to the memory of Roy Honeyman; and to the warm memory of my father, Bernard Goodman, who started it all by being such a magical telephone communicator and special human being.

Contents

Preface

Opportunity Doesn't Knock Anymore—It Phones!™

In a recent issue of our nationally distributed *Telephone Effectiveness Newsletter,* we ran an article that asked, "Is the Traveling Salesman Coming to the End of the Road?" The answer to that question is "yes." With the time, fuel, and money crunches we have all faced in the past ten years, fewer and fewer companies can afford to put salespeople in the field when the average cost of an industrial sales visit is between $160 and $300.

This doesn't mean that all salespeople will become obsolete, but it clearly tells us that we need to exploit the most logical substitute for face-to-face calls—which is, of course, the telephone. This book is geared to helping you to become comfortable with a professional approach to tele-marketing known as the Goodman Method™, which has been tested over fourteen years in every major industry in America.

One day soon, our customers will start *demanding* a low-cost alternative to the personal sales visit, because they will know that they are paying a huge premium for the luxury of "pressing the flesh" and meeting us in person. A well-conducted presentation can not only take the place of time-wasting visits, but it can put more money in our pockets by giving us more *selling time*, rather than "windshield time," and waiting time.

You're going to like this book! I know this because it has been "written" by thousands of your most successful peers in America who have attended my training seminars over the past several years. Their wisdom will be yours after you have completed this book. You will be better able to open calls smoothly, close effectively, manage resistance and objections, understand the psychological hurdles of telemarketing, as well as manage others. More important, you will like and respect the telephone more as your tool of choice rather than necessity in selling.

You probably have a lot of questions about this book and about telemarketing particularly. I hope you'll look through the first chapter of the book right away, "The Thirty Most-Asked Questions About Telemarketing and Management." I'm confident you'll see some new and interesting answers to some of your questions.

The remainder of the book is dedicated to the essence of the Goodman System™, which is designed to help you pick up the phone, and reach out and sell someone!

ACKNOWLEDGMENTS

I owe a debt of gratitude to the thousands of clients, customers, and seminar attendees who have seen fit to honor and support me through the years with their generous patronage. They are the ones who grant me the continuing privilege to do the things I like best: to perform, sell, think, write, and learn. They serve as some of my finest teachers.

The scores of universities, professional associations, and companies that have sponsored my customer relations, selling skills, and telemarketing and management seminars should be thanked as well.

I would also like to thank my wife, critic, and friend, Deanne, for her supportiveness and continuing inspiration.

And I would like to extend a special word of appreciation to Alexander Graham Bell, originally a speech teacher, who had a better idea and the courage and vision to put it to work.

REACH OUT
& SELL
SOMEONE

chapter one

The thirty most-asked questions about telemarketing and management

Most people who purchase books on particular subjects such as telemarketing have a few pet questions that they would like to have answered. Armed with these questions they frantically search through the table of contents and then the subject index at the end of the book to determine if the writer is going to address the matters at all. The last recourse, naturally, is to wade through chapter after chapter in a long search for particulars.

The format of this book is different. Much of this work has been fashioned after the Telephone Marketing and Management and Customer Relations seminars that I present across the country. In these programs we have a unit on troubleshooting, in which I spend a considerable amount of time addressing specific questions from the audience. Because you can't really interact with me on that sort of basis through a book, I am going to try to supply an alternative arrangement.

I am going to furnish the thirty questions most-asked in my seminars in order to give you an initial glimpse of my philosophy of telemarketing, as well as to save you time in finding matters of immediate importance to you. Many of these topics are covered in greater detail in the remaining chapters of the book. Some of the questions will be so specific as to merit only a short response.

I hope you will be sufficiently moved by this overture to stay for the rest of the symphony. If you are standing in a bookstore reading these words, I hope this beginning will be of help in your buying decision.

Question #1:   *Why are the people who call me at home so obnoxious?*

It's true that most of the calls we receive from telephone salespeople are painful exercises in restraint, at least on our part. I am the first to admit that most telephone solicitors are terrible communicators. They treat us as if we are "buying objects," who have been trained only to say yes when it is our brief time to talk within the context of the planned presentation. Why are these folks so bad? They are either (1) untrained, or (2) poorly trained.

As I write these words, I am returning from answering a poorly delivered telephone pitch that went as follows: "Hello, my name is Mary Smith, and I'm with Acme Carpet Cleaning, and I'd like to know if we can come by and give you an estimate on cleaning your carpet?" You might ask, "What's wrong with that pitch?" Well, it really doesn't *sell* any benefits, and it has obviously been designed for the operator to use hundreds of times a day. Moreover, it literally *asks us to reject the caller* because the request for an estimate sounds so weak.

This call is mild when compared to numbers of others whose makers are abusive and antagonistic with us when we deny their request for action.

Question #2:   *You're not going to make me sound like one of them, are you?*

No. The techniques in this book have been tested and proven effective with all sorts of people and are seldom considered offensive. In fact, one of the basic tenets of my telephone selling philosophy is that *there is a tomorrow*, and what we say to a customer today and how we treat that person will be revisited upon us later.

Question #3:   *What is a telephone sale, anyway?*

I define a telephone sale very broadly to include all commercial persuasive efforts made by phone. This means that if we call someone because we want them to purchase carpet cleaning services, we are selling. If we simply answer an incoming call as a receptionist, we are also selling in the sense that we are trying to *persuade* the customer to think well of our firm and to be favorably predisposed toward doing business with us. In other words, our receptionist may be selling existing customers on taking their business elsewhere, merely by sounding caustic or impatient or indifferent. A client of mine in the electronics field discovered to his amazement that the number one complaint against his company came as a result of the poor manner with which incoming callers were handled by the receptionist.

In short, *all* calls are sales efforts, and we are all salespeople, by virtue of the fact that we are continuously trying to persuade others to think or act toward us in a particular manner.

Question #4:   *Aren't most people reluctant to make purchases by telephone?*

Selling by telephone is a nine billion dollar industry and growing rapidly, according to *The Wall Street Journal*. The explosion in the use of 800 phone numbers is truly amazing. I was looking at the back of a package of Northern bathroom tissue the other day and noticed the line, "If you have any questions about our product, call 1-800-243-5384." I can't imagine why they would need an 800 number, yet consumers are apparently getting so used toll-free calling conveniences that the firm thought it should have one to keep up with the times.

Making purchases by phone is now seen as a convenience by shoppers who want to order merchandise from department stores without the hassle of finding parking spaces in crowded downtown areas or malls. The phone is also the fastest way of pinpointing customers who most want to know about special sales or bargains as they appear. Because we are all facing energy, time, and money crunches, the consumer and businessperson are coming to recognize that the phone is a very valuable tool to use to keep cost pressures down as well as to take advantage of new opportunities.

Some folks do suffer from "phone fear," as we have reported in the *Telephone Effectiveness Newsletter* we publish. They are afraid of speaking to others on the phone and are reluctant to make purchasing decisions through this device. Such persons are statistically rare compared to the great number who will consent to an appeal made by telephone.

There are people who attend my seminars and flatly claim "I never buy anything by phone," to which I respond, "Have you ever ordered a pizza or started a magazine subscription by phone?" They usually concede that they may have done so once or twice, but insist that they wanted the items. This is precisely what a salesperson is trained to do, to make us believe we are *buying* instead of *being sold*.

Question #5:   *Are males or females better at selling on the phone?*

The answer to this question depends on a number of factors. What are they selling? I know some females who are having a very tough time selling "macho" items such as industrial tools, while others report that some of their male customers are thrilled to be speaking to a female instead of the "hard-bitten" males they are accustomed to dealing with. There are certain products that are classically associated with femininity, such as household cleaning services, baby supplies, family photographs and portraits, and the like. Females selling these products to females may obtain the best results. When I was with Time/Life Books, we sold several libraries on various subjects. The "Old West Library" seemed to sell faster when men were doing the pitching, while the "Library of Art" was a lively seller for female reps.

The rise of feminism, and the fact that more and more influential businesspersons are female makes using a female to sell other females sound advice. There seems to be a code of supportiveness between females who encounter each other in industry these days. When I was experiencing difficulties selling services to particular females in the past, I would ask my female associate, Dr. Deanne Honeyman-Goodman to come into the proceedings. Invariably, she would be able to interact smoothly with females with whom I felt I was clashing. She would also be able to verify or disconfirm my perceptions that the other party was acting defensively toward me.

Only yesterday, I was speaking with a veteran in telemarketing who vowed that he wouldn't hire one more male because he felt that males in a telephone sales room spent too much time boasting and "strutting like peacocks," as he put it. Females, on the other hand, did not seem to produce as many orders in the short run, but their reliability was much higher Their level of absenteeism was less than that of males, and they seemed to work harder, according to this veteran's report.

When my firm, Goodman Communications, was performing marketing research by phone, we found that females were better able to get sensitive information and intelligence from male sources than were males talking to males. Perhaps males thought that other males were more likely to pose a threat to their business interests than were females.

It should be noted that there are always exceptions. I know some females who sell "macho products" like nobody's business, and males who are superb at articulating the benefits of so-called feminine products. The best method to use is to test the subject for yourself by having a *split-test*. Use both males and females and measure the success of each group with particular products and clients over time. This is truly the most reliable method of determining the impact of gender upon telemarketing performance.

Question #6:   *What do you think of "music-on-hold"?*

It depends on the song they're playing. If I like it, okay. If their selection doesn't coincide with my taste, they may be in trouble. Unfortunately, music is a very personal thing. Some folks would love to listen to the Rolling Stones while holding for five or ten minutes, while others would be thrilled at the tones of Luciano Pavarotti. By using music, you're going to offend somebody.

I enjoy listening to the news when I'm holding, but some customers of yours would probably find this depressing. There is another danger in using news-on-hold. Your competitors may discover that you are tuned to a particular station and decide to saturate the station with their advertising. This danger also exists if you elect to use a commercial music station.

Question #7:   *How can I break through a secretary's screening efforts?*

To sell somebody something, we have to first get the person's attention. When there is a "lion at the gate" in the form of a secretary or screener, this task becomes more challenging. There is one simple suggestion when confronting any obstacle: we can go through it, above it, beneath it, or around it. Here's how this process works when dealing with screening.

Most of us are sitting ducks for screeners. We call and ask, "Is Mary Jones there?" to which we hear two questions in reply. "Who is calling, please" is the first query, followed soon thereafter by, "And may I ask what this is regarding?" One way to derail this sort of probe is by announcing who we are and what we want *before the person can screen us out.* "Hello, Dr. Goodman calling for Mary Jones about our correspondence. Thank you." This tells the screener that we are so confident that we can announce ourselves without fear of rejection and that we belong to the privileged who should be channeled directly to Ms. Jones' sanctum without further ado. By punctuating my announcement with the words, "Thank you," I am rather smoothly saying, "Now, put me through without any further delay, you Bozo!"

What if the screener is particularly "sporting" that day, and decides to be a little more resistant to our charms, and asks, "And what was the specific nature of your correspondence?" We will then need to *go through the obstacle* by *overinvesting* the screener with authority. "Oh," we will gleefully reply, "I'm sure you can help me with that. We were discussing the financial needs of your firm, and I needed to find out, before we proceed further, what the annual revenues of your company were for last year. You should have the figure handy, am I right?" Instantly, you will hear the reply of someone who is in over his or her head. The response will be "Oh, no, um, uh, you'll have to talk with Ms. Jones about that. I'll put you right through."

With particularly stodgy or large companies with many levels of screeners, I suggest you *go above the anticipated obstacle* before you confront it by calling a superior of the person with whom you wish to speak. You won't be able to talk with that party either, but this isn't your purpose anyway. Call the president's secretary and ask this person whom you should speak to in the organization about such-and-such a matter. If he or she balks, you might have the name handy of the person you are going to call, and inquire, "Would Harry Frisbee be likely to handle this?" The secretary may say you might try him first. Your next step is to call Frisbee's secretary and say, "Hello, this is Dr. Goodman calling for Mr. Frisbee at the request of Mr. President's office. Thank you." Most secretaries will not have the impertinence to inquire further as to what the matter refers. When you reach the party you wish, say, "Mr. So-and-so's assistant suggested I contact you about such-and-such." This will give your sales call the ring of authority and the credibility of a third-party referral.

One of the ways to *go beneath the obstacle* is to make friends with the principal's secretary. Let's say that you have been trying to no avail to get through to a person for days. Each time you call you hear, "I'm sorry, she's in a meeting." What can you do? I suggest you ask for the secretary's name and ask her, in a very friendly, off the record tone, "When is the best time to reach Ms. Jones?" If the secreary claims ignorance, press further by offering a choice close: "Most busy executives like Ms. Jones tend to come to the office really early in the morning to organize their day, or they stay late. Which would be a better time to speak to her for just a few minutes?" You may find that the secretary reveals something to you that she was supposed to keep quiet. She might say, "Well, she comes in around 7 A.M., and you can probably reach her then. But, don't tell her I told you to call!" By making friends with the screener we are also able to enjoy the persuasive powers such persons have over their principals. Screeners, who are in our corner might say to the boss, "This nice woman is on the line from Groton's. Do you have a quick minute for her?" which is a lot more appealing than, "The lady from Groton's is on the line, again! What should I tell her?"

Going around the obstacle would be accomplished by calling someone else in the target organization who does not answer directly to the person with whom you want to speak. For instance, you might call someone in customer service if you want to learn when to place a call to catch the sales manager for a few minutes. You'll be amazed at the details you can get from third parties who are a bit removed from the principal.

Question #8:   *When I answer the phone, should I say this is "Sherri" or "Sherri Smith" or "Ms. Smith"?*

I believe we should answer the phone with dignity. This does not mean that we should sound off-putting or haughty, but friendly *and* professional. I think that answering the phone with a first name only tends to make us sound like we are children. "Hello, Goodman residence. James, speaking." I prefer to use *both* first and last name when we are inviting the caller to use either in addressing us. If we are trying to create distance between ourselves and our clients, as is the case in a number of organizations, I suggest the use of a title, such as "Dr.," "Mr.," or "Ms.," followed by the last name.

If you are uncertain how to address someone else, I suggest you use a title and the person's last name until invited to do otherwise. If the person knows you are on a line, and she picks up her phone and says, "Hello, this is Mary," don't revert to the formal salutation and call her Ms. Jones.

By the way, when addressing females over the phone in the formal mode, I suggest you always use "Ms.," because it sounds like "Ms." as well as a slurred "Mrs." Either way, you win!

Question #9: *What do you think of telephone answering machines?*

Machines can be a lot better than some of the live answering services that I have had recent dealings with. One of the obvious plusses of a machine is that it records exactly what was said, without distortion. Humans have a tendency to alter what they have heard and transcribe the wrong message. Moreover, if you are like me, you are probably interested in knowing how the caller sounded when she left the message. Many people are ill-equipped to describe voices, while a machine can play a voice back to us over and over until we derive a clear perception of the attitude of the caller. When negotiating, this information is particularly valuable.

One of the negative aspects of using a machine is that some callers will be self-conscious about the quality of their voices and will hang up instead of leaving a message. This can be frustrating for both parties. Others who try to reach you several times during a particular period may be hesitant to leave a number of messages because they don't wish to appear overly anxious about reaching you.

When it comes to a well-trained machine versus a poorly trained human, I'll take the machine. It's also cheaper, and it never takes a coffee break.

As machines come into greater home and office use, acceptance of them will increase.

Question #10: *Which is a more effective medium: direct mail or tele-marketing?*

I use both methods a great deal to market services and products. I like direct mail because it is more scientific, in most applications, in determining the relative impact of sales upon purchasers. In addition, you can show the buyer photos or drawings of the product, whereas this is impossible, at present, by phone.

Telemarketing is a better method to *test* an offer because it yields data immediately. It is also a dynamic medium because it can be suited to each prospect as an individual during the cut and thrust of a call. Because a phone call is a more personal medium of communication, it is more difficult to avoid, especially if we receive it at home. As a result, the proportion of sales made to presentations offered will be much higher over the phone.

The best of both worlds is to *combine* direct mail with telemarketing to appeal to as many sensory modalities in the prospect as possible. As we will note in Chapter Four, The Anatomy of a Sales Call, a before-mailing approach as well as after-mailing approach can be very successfully employed in telemarketing. A telephone follow-up to a direct mail offering may yield ten times the result of direct mail alone.

Question #11: *When is the best time to call consumers at home?*

Dinnertime. That's when they're at home. "But, aren't people likely to be upset over having their dinner disturbed?" some of you may ask. A surprisingly small percentage of the people who are called at home between the hours of 5 and 9 P.M. express negative attitudes. In fact, in my personal experience, only one out of about every five-hundred responded negatively to a call during those hours.

The next best time to reach consumers is during the early morning hours, before they have embarked on chores away from home. The doldrums for making contacts come in the afternoon.

Question #12:   *When is the best time to call businesses?*

Research has shown that there are two peak periods of telephone activity during the business day: 11:30 in the morning and 2:30 in the afternoon. This means that most telephone contacts are being made during these times. In general, then, it would follow that you will find the average person available for a call at these times.

Few people are average, though. Doctors are difficult to reach from the early hours of the morning until the late afternoon, and may not be available at all on some days. Schoolteachers would tend to be unavailable during the peak traffic hours mentioned above.

I find that it is helpful to reach people at the beginning of their business day. This means that if I am calling from California to Chicago, I am going to get up a few hours early to reach my counterparts at 8:30 or 9:00 A.M., *their* time. They usually marvel at my verve to be calling at 6:30 or so, Pacific Time. When I reach folks at the start of day they seem to be fresh and haven't had a chance to have their day ruined by other callers or office problems. This makes them more receptive to my message.

As I mentioned in my other book, *Winning by Telephone,** setting up *telephone appointments* to reach busy executives is a handy practice. In this fashion we determine in advance with the other party or her assistant when a good time will be to call. This is then noted on the calendars of both parties, and the resulting call is treated with the same respect and seriousness as would a personal, face-to-face meeting.

One of the main gripes of telephone marketers is that they are calling people "at a lousy time." This may be true, in some cases, but it is a more creative and useful idea to think that "there are no better times than the present in which to make a sale." Armed with this thought, we should be prepared to do well on all occasions.

Question #13:   *What can you say to customers who ask you to go out on a date?*

Yes or no. In all seriousness, though, this does pose a problem for a number of folks who would like a delicate way to handle would-be suitors.

---

*Gary S. Goodman, *Winning by Telephone: Telephone Effectiveness for Business Professionals and Consumers* (Englewood Cliffs, N. J.: Prentice-Hall, Inc., 1982).

Think about it: we're in a bind, because we are supposed to be friendly with customers who are said to always be right. At least, this is the company line in most places. What happens when friendliness spills over into something else, or when a customer thinks there is whoopee in our tone of voice?

I suggest we lie, if we have to. To reply to a request for a date, "Well, thank you, but I'm spoken for already," and then get back to business, is okay. Or to say, "My wife wouldn't take too well to that idea," might be acceptable, even if we are unmarried. Persistent bozos have been known to retort, "Well, bring her along!"

Another approach is to flatly state that you would like to keep the relationship on a business level. This may be true, but it sounds like a brushoff and may be taken personally.

Question # 14: *What if you want to develop sales resistance and fight back against telephone calls made to you?*

Read this book. All of the tools and techniques that are used by the offensive team may be employed successfully by the defensive team.

Question #15: *How long should the average telephone sales call last?*

How long should the tail of a dog be? It should fit the dog, and the same "appropriateness" standard applies to a phone presentation. If you are performing a good amount of qualifying of the needs of the prospect, and the call takes on an interview format, it will last longer than a sales appeal geared to making the same pitch to an entire class of people.

On the whole, however, it is wise to remember that the average adult attention span is said to be about *four seconds long*! Brevity is essential. Many presentations can last from one and one-half to three minutes in length, and still keep the party awake and interested.

I have used a presentation in the past that lasts only twenty seconds, yet is followed by a confirmation of particulars that takes about five minutes to transact. Assent was achieved after the first few seconds, though.

Question #16:   *How many sales contacts may be made during an hour of calling?*

This depends upon a number of factors, including the length of each call made. The time of day will inform how many sales presentations may be made. Fewer contacts will occur in the afternoons, for example. Who are you calling? Do these people answer their own lines, or do secretaries screen callers before putting the calls through?

I have been associated with telemarketing efforts where the average number of contacts per hour was as high as twenty. The number of *completed presentations*, where a yes or no answer was obtained, was about eight. Six said no at the end of the pitch, and two said yes. Remember, I am speaking here of a statistical average, when consumers were called at all hours of the day and where the presentation lasted, on the average, less than two minutes.

If you are supervising others I suggest you determine for yourself how many contacts should be made and request evidence from employees that they are, indeed, making that number. Reps may be asked to keep running tallies to assist this effort. When you have determined averages, you will be in a good position to construct a reward system based upon realistic expectations.

Question #17:   *If we take incoming calls, should we screen them, even if we risk offending the customer?*

If screening serves a legitimate function, and it is performed professionally, it is entirely acceptable from my point of view. Most screening is poorly done, however. It sounds as if we are interrogating the caller. "Who's calling???" is a very harsh way of determining who is on the line. There are several acceptable alternatives such as "May I ask your name, please?" or "May I ask the name of your firm, please?" or even, "May I reference this call for you?" The last phrase is used quite successfully by staffers at IBM, and I think it sounds great, although it takes a little getting used to saying smoothly.

If screening is used merely "to sound like we're a professional office," and you are going to accept all calls, irrespective of who is on the line, I suggest you forget about screening. The customer will recognize that he was put through hoops needlessly, and will resent the exercise.

Question #18:   *If I am hiring others to do calling for me, who are the best people to hire?*

The most successful telephone marketers are not typical, average Americans. They are different from most folks. They can handle rejection better, and have what I term *performative discipline*. They also are trained to accept criticism more gracefully than the rest of us and can act upon the new directions swiftly and efficiently.

Who are these people? What sorts of people should I avoid? These questions are addressed in detail in Chapter Six of this book.

Question #19:   *My local telephone company says it will help me to start a telemarketing program. What will they do for me?*

I can't speak for all telephone companies, now or in the future, but I can safely say that most phone companies are not experts in the *human side* of telemarketing. They will help you to buy hardware and long distance services, which are their stock and trade. They will also offer advice which is designed to whet your appetite for buying what they *really* have to offer, such as WATS lines, elaborate PBXs, and the like.

Like many firms, the phone company will sell you as much as it can of certain products and services, whether or not such quantities or items are necessary to your business. A client of mine in a prestigious firm in Indiana reported to me that one phone company proposed to sell the firm twenty WATS lines to *test* a telemarketing program. I was asked if that was an appropriate suggestion. I replied that a real test could be accomplished with a few regular lines over a relatively short time, with minimal out-of-pocket expense. If WATS lines were then determined necessary, I suggested they be considered at that time.

Some telemarketing consultants suggest that phone companies cannot be relied on to give meaningful training in the area of selling by phone because the folks doing the training have not had to compete in the marketplace or the real world until recently.

Question #20:   *Should there be a dress code in a telephone marketing office?*

There are two schools of thought on this issue:

1. Folks behave in a manner consistent with the clothing they are wearing. Put them in shorts and tee shirts, and they'll act like they are on vacation, and put them in ties and dresses and they'll act like mature businesspeople.
2. What difference does it make how they look, nobody can see them.

I tend to side with the second school. One of the main perquisites or "perks" of a telephone marketing job is the fact that one may feel looser in a phone room while meeting customers electronically rather than face to face. The only real impression we have to make is with our voices and knowledge, which may be communicated without reference to attire.

Some folks feel confined in a telephone atmosphere unless they are given ways to feel a sense of freedom. I think clothing is one area of individual choice that I would allow the employee to govern.

If customers can actually see the reps, this may require stricter standards than otherwise. One very large and successful tire company that subscribes to our Telephone Effectiveness Newsletter reports that it provides telemarketers with their own exclusive entrance to the building in order to separate them from others who might be put off by their appearance.

You will also want to consider allowing for diversity in clothing styles based upon the types of people I will be suggesting you hire when this subject is covered in Chapter Six.

Question #21: *Should we use calling scripts or canned presentations?*

Patterned sales presentations form the basis of all significant telemarketing programs. This means that firms that are most successful realize that their good fortune is attributable not to luck or to the fact that they have been blessed with the presence of sales geniuses, but rather that their high sales come from a refined *routine* that their telemarketers are required to follow.

We can't worship at the altar of spontaneity if we really want to be regarded as professionals. Our sales approach needs to be calculated in advance to produce certain effects upon listeners.

There is a fundamental maxim about human behavior that needs to be noted: *All that is natural is not all that is good.* In other words, it may be natural for us to sleep all day, but who would pay the bills? A successful telemarketing program employs people who have skills in using the right *trained response* at the correct point in a sales call. This idea will be amplified in Chapter Five on the Telephone Sales Canons, and in Chapter Six on the Anatomy of a Sales Call.

Question #22: *Is telephone language different from face-to-face language?*

Yes, and it's important to realize this point and to plan our telephone calls accordingly. When we greet a customer or prospect face-to-face, we may luxuriate in the fact that the other person will be setting aside a certain amount of time for us, and even if we are particularly long-winded, he or she will probably find it difficult to disengage the contact gracefully.

On the phone, the person is much more likely to bring the call to a conclusion if she feels it isn't going anywhere. In addition, the client is heir to thousands of office distractions that can impede our telephone talk. Therefore, we need to manage time better when making a presentation through this device.

We also need to be crucially aware of certain "weasel words" or "devil terms" that can creep into a call and ruin our sales efforts. Words such as "if" and "I'd like to" are particularly weak and tend to induce the contact to reject our appeal.

We need to limit the number of product features and benefits that we refer to when speaking on the phone. This will be discussed further in Chapter Four.

Question #23:   *If we are sending a product to a customer on approval, how can we make sure he or she will give it serious consideration, and not simply return it or keep it without paying for it?*

There is no complete defense against dishonesty, but we can very often assess the seriousness of a potential buyer by asking what I call a "bottom line qualifying question." I usually like to ask such a customer, "If you like the product, will you buy it?" This tends to produce the clarity we are after by insisting upon a yes or no answer at the end of the call. The same type of phrase may be used to answer the objection of someone who insists, "I don't really think I'll be interested in what your selling," by asking, "If I can save you money, will you be interested in trying the service?" This is an if-then question format that works very well in determining whether a prospect will give our cause a fair appraisal.

Question #24:   *What sort of voice works best for selling by telephone?*

In the 1950s, having an English accent was all the rage. In fact, as I understand it, executives in large Eastern cities competed with each other in trying to hire someone who could sound a little snootier than the secretary next door. If you look at movies from that period you will note that the actors who were very successful seemed to possess an upper crust accent that might have originated in Britain or New England.

Today, such artificial standards for judging dialect seem to be falling by the wayside. People are proud of their Southern, Western, and Eastern accents, and want to hear themselves played back to themselves when they speak on the phone. In other words, we respond favorably to most people when they sound like we do. This suggests that telecommunicators should cultivate the art of *code-switching*, or adjusting their voices to blend with the other parties with thom they are speaking. On one call, a telemarketer might sound like he or she is from Texas, and on another, from Maine, depending upon the voice on the other end. In *Winning by Telephone*, I point out how code switching is best accomplished as a method of helping us to sound credible before people from all different regions.

We do wish to avoid hiring folks who have acute vocal damage, or who have particularly unpleasant voices to listen to. At the same time, we don't have to sound like radio announcers to be successful, either.

Question #25:   *How long can we expect the average telemarketing rep to stay on the job?*

One thing that people discover when they implement telemarketing programs is that they don't resemble the Civil Service in regard to stable employment patterns. In fact, in most phone rooms, employee turnover reaches epidemic proportions.

Why is this so? First of all, telemarketing candidates are not sufficiently screened in advance to weed out those who will definitely fail. Some folks are simply poor risks to bring aboard to begin with. The job, is also a villain. Few can sustain the energy and fortitude necessary to deal with the typical telemarketing job on a day-to-day basis.

Some folks will "dial and smile" for about two hours before they tell you the job is not right for them. This hurts, when we consider that it may have cost us hundreds of dollars in time and advertising to bring the person in for a trial. Others, who are better equipped to handle telemarketing, will stay with a firm for as many as a few years or more.

I am suspicious of firms that claim they have cured the turnover problem. They have made some compromises somewhere if this is the case. (See Chapter Six.)

Question #26: *Should incoming calls be handled differently than outgoing calls?*

I believe there is too much made of the presumed distinction between inbound and outbound telemarketing. Just because somebody *called us* should not revolutionize the way we manage that call versus the outgoing one. For instance, if we are well trained, we will handle the incoming call with the same sort of style and commitment to closing with which we would make the outgoing cold call. Unfortunately, most folks aren't trained this way. They are taught to allow the incoming caller to set the agenda for the call and control the conversation thereafter. This foolishly results in lost sales, and personnel who consider themselves order-takers instead of order-*makers*.

Some people insist that if someone calls us, they are definitely interested in what we are selling so all we need to do is let the party buy. Oh, if life were only so easy! A good number of folks who call any business *don't know what they want, nor what they should buy*. Consequently, they need to be *guided* in their decision making by skilled telephone operators or marketers. We should be vigilant in assuring that those who handle incoming calls are capable of gently terminating long-winded callers for the purpose of reducing the average length and cost of calls.

In Chapter Four, we will demonstrate how the anatomy of a sales call can be used effectively in managing both inbound and outbound calls.

Question #27:   *How can we get lonely people off the line without offending them?*

Many of us have certain clients who gravitate toward us because they know we're polite and will let them ramble on about their recent fishing trip or their grandchildren or their most recent picnic. A certain amount of small talk is helpful in a sales call, but too often we can become victimized by our own good manners and courtesy shown to the blabberers of the world.

How, then, may we swiftly terminate calls with such folks? I suggest you study the list of transition phrases to be found in Chapter Five of this book. These phrases will help you to reassert control over the call when you've temporarily lost it. I suggest you bolster your inventory of "little lies" to include the oldie, "Well, I'm sorry, but I have another call," and "I have another person on hold who I really should get to," or other lines such as these. Who can hate you for having to attend to other pressing business?

We should also remember that closing a call, in any circumstance, is very similar to closing a sale. In fact, the next time a blabberer runs away with a call, use the assumptive-checkback close to be found in Chapter Four. You'll love it.

Question #28:   *Can outside salespeople be converted easily into inside salespeople or telemarketers?*

Not without a lot of screaming and kicking. At least at first. Here is the typical scenario. A company decides to cut costs by bringing an experienced "roadie" like Harry in from the field, where he has been stationed for some twenty years. He feels a little shortchanged, because he won't have an expense account anymore. He also won't have any need for that nice sedan and the free insurance that comes with it. He also won't have to worry about those idle spins down highways only to discover that his contact stepped out for a few hours, because he'll only be a finger-walk away from speaking with the next person on the phone. Anyway, he *won't be allowed* to be bored because his supervisor will be breathing down his neck at each moment. Moreover, he won't need those fat commissions that he used to get almost as combat pay for being on the road, away from the family. We'll put him on a salary, and make a company man out of him yet!

Get the picture? From old Harry's point of view, taking a telemarketing assignment may be like volunteering for imprisonment. Based upon the relatively cushy life he once led, the new post seems like a disaster.

To acclimate a roadie to the rigors of telemarketing may require a significant amount of reeduction. He or she will be extremely sensitive to any sacrifices that the company is requesting in terms of relinquished perks. If we hope to keep the person employed with us, we may be wise to show how he or she may *fare better under telemarketing*. This will lower the threat threshold and seem a little more motivational to the person than any alternatives.

I have encountered exceptions to this process of alienation. When an outside salesperson is brought inside to handle accounts with which he had already been familiar, this can work out well. He still needs to be instructed in how to cultivate relationships exclusively by phone, though.

Question #29:   *Can inside salespeople become good outside salespeople?*

Yes. They seem to adapt well to moving out of doors. They also tend to go for the jugular in closing sales swiftly and in trying to manage time effectively. *Good* telemarketers, however, get frustrated easily with many of the wasteful rituals involved in outside sales. The first thing they'll ask for is a phone for the car so they can call ahead to clients to make sure they will be there upon arrival.

Question #30:   *With so many companies rushing into telemarketing,*
what will this mean for the typical rep on the phone?

Telephone marketers are simply going to have to become more sophisticated in how they handle their communications with clients and prospects.
They are going to be competing with a number of other callers for the
attention of the same potential buyers. Sales appeals that are based upon
greed, fear, and high pressure are going to be increasingly resented. Selling
by phone will have to be based upon solid principles of human communication that have been derived from research and state-of-the-art analysis. The
key to survival and prosperity will be based upon how the telemarketer
may make his or her approach sound distinctive and professional.

This will also be good for those who decide to go into telemarketing. I already hear from those who are looking for "really good" telephone
communicators and managers to fill attractive positions. With more job
openings, and few capably trained people to fill them, salaries have to
move in an upward direction for experienced professionals.

As you move through the remaining chapters of this book you will
find answers to other questions you may have, as well as explicit instruc-
tions in such areas as understanding the psychology of telemarketing; the
telephone sales canons or tips for preparing telemarketing procedures;
the four-part structure for organizing the anatomy of a sales call; methods
for effectively handling resistance and objections; and how to manage the
human side of telemarketing.

These will provide you with an understanding of the Goodman
System of telemarketing and management.

chapter two

The psychology of telemarketing

Many extremely capable sales and marketing professionals will not make it in a telemarketing atmosphere. In fact, they may encounter their own professional equivalent of Napolean's Waterloo. Why will they fail?

Some people will be forced to retreat from this dynamic marketing medium because they and their staff are unprepared to handle the inner challenges of telemarketing. To put it succinctly, the greatest threshold to be crossed will be psychological in character. Unless we are prepared to negotiate psychological hazards that block the path to success, we will not realize the vast potential of telemarketing. What are some of the processes we need to be cautioned against?

I HATE THOSE PEOPLE WHO CALL ME AT HOME, AND I REFUSE TO BE ONE OF THEM!

We all have had the unpleasant experience of rushing to answer our home telephone only to discover that on the other end someone is droning at us about some obscure magazine or home improvement offer. Many of us will wait patiently until the message has concluded, to reply with a cool, "I'm not interested."

It is unfortunate that telephone marketing has suffered from a poor image in the marketplace, largely as a result of the unskilled people who have called households in the past. Many of these solicitors have been given a poorly constructed pitch to read and have been given little or no training. They either sink or swim, and we, the receivers of the sales appeals, often go down with the ship as well.

Many of the phone rooms in which such people work are supervised by people who want to rack up sales at any cost. They will not be concerned if they offend half of the people with whom they speak if the other half can be convinced to hear the entire pitch and possibly buy.

This is probably *not* the sort of operation that you are going to be a part of, yet there is always the concern we have that we will be judged to be just like the unprofessionals who are also using the telephone to market product and services. It is the fear of association that keeps us from exploiting the telephone for our own professional purposes. What we need to remember, and what will become even more clear as you move through this book, is that you are not going to sound like the ill-trained bozos who call folks at home. You will be better prepared to share the conversation with the prospect, as well as to be sensitive to his or her attitudes and needs. By coming across as a mature telemarketer, you will avoid the stigma of the typical solicitor.

MYTHS ABOUT SELLING BY TELEPHONE

There are several untruths that are perpetuated about selling by telephone. By examining these, we should be able to be liberated from them.

Myth #1:   *There are certain things that simply can't be sold by phone!*

This fiction is usually uttered by salespeople who aren't any good on the telephone themselves, and who misunderstand the power of the medium. They would be surprised at how much can be accomplished by creative telemarketers. For instance, when I was in the automotive leasing business several years ago, my sales manager thought I was foolish to be using the phone for prospecting. He thought I should have been knocking on doors. After I quickly turned in my first deals made by phone, he installed an entire telemarketing function in the office! If we don't try to realize the full potential of the phone, we can be assured that our competitors will.

Myth #2:   *The telephone is a much less intimate means to meet and greet people than being in their physical presence.*

It is certainly true that being in another's presence can be more fulfilling, at certain times, than speaking with the person on the phone. Nonetheless, most of us can be a lot more friendly on the phone than we think. Because we are not looking the other person right in the eye when we are on the phone, many of us fail to *try* to be warm and cordial. We suffer from split personalities, in which we are very outgoing in person, yet quite reserved and even cold when we speak on the phone. In person we use an exciting voice, and on the phone we use a monotone. This unnecessary difference can be remedied with effort applied to our telephone effectiveness.

Myth #3:   *People have to look us in the eye to trust us.*

This may be the case for some people who are phone-shy or who have been burned by telephonic misrepresentations in the past. Most people, however, are surprisingly receptive to reasonable appeals made by phone. There are some subtle things we can do to overcome a buyer's reluctance and establish credibility and trust. As I mention in my book *Winning by Telephone*, we need to build trust by self-disclosing, code-switching, and echoing certain terms that are used by the prospect. We'll briefly explain these concepts in order.

Prospects need to trust people from whom they are buying. How can a prospect determine if a person on the other end of the phone is trust-worthy? The voice is really the only thing the prospect has by which to make a judgment. He or she cannot *see* if we are okay, so this fact is to be inferred, based upon what we say and how we say it. I suggest you set the prospect at ease by telling the prospect who you are before he has to ask you.

In addition, you will want to tell the other person a little about yourself, rather than keep yourself a mystery. You might comment on the "great weather we're having," or the fact that the local sports team is doing very well. This sort of small talk, in the proper measure, will tell the other person that you are like him or her, which is what the person needs to conclude if trust is to be created. Another thing to do is *blend your voice with the other person's,* and try to sound like he or she does. If you are speaking from the Northeast with someone from the South, you may find that your prospect is speaking slower than you are. That's okay. Simply slow your rate to conform more closely with the other person's. Similarly, if the other voice is softer, don't make yours big and booming. Instead, reduce your volume. This is called code-switching, and it really tends to put the other party at ease. Don't overdo it, though. You are not supposed to be thought of as a mimic or impressionist. You should also listen to the prospect for certain *key terms* that she uses. If she uses *visual* phrases, such as, "*Look* at it from my point of *view,*" or "I *see* it this way," don't speak to her from a *tactile* mode by insisting, "But, this is how I *feel* about the matter," or "Let's get a *handle* on this thing." These would be "touch-words," and would make the prospect feel estranged from you. In other words, try to key in on the types of *sensory* terms that are being used, and *echo* these back to the other person. It will appear that you are speaking the other person's language, which is a good way to create identification, trust, and credibility.

Myth #4:   *There isn't enough time to make a strong case on the phone.*

Many salespeople use overkill in selling. They give the client too much information, which encourages the client to see more problems in the proposal than he or she would have seen otherwise. One of the best suggestions for salespeople is to "keep it simple, salesperson," or the so-called *kiss* method of selling. In other words, if we make things too complicated, we will talk our way out of a deal. By using the phone, we are compelled to be concise, and there is a built-in governor on our desire to ramble.

People are also known to have very short attention spans, and it behooves us to state our cases clearly and briefly for this reason.

Myth #5: *It may be okay to use the phone for a quick sale, but you can't build a long lasting relationship with a customer by phone.*

This is an assertion that is made frequently by those who attend our Telephone Marketing and Management seminars around the country. It is false because countless firms open accounts by telephone and sustain business relationships with the same clients *without ever seeing the people face-to-face.* In fact, the telephone is a much more appropriate medium for just saying hello, or for just seeing how your stock is holding up, than getting into a gas and time guzzler and motoring off to eyeball the client and stock for ourselves.

Myth #6: *If our company uses the phone to sell a client, and our competitor continues to visit the client, our competitor will have the edge over us and get the business.*

This fear prevents many organizations from embracing the phone as a marketing tool. IBM seems to have come up with a solution. In ads that have run in the *Wall Street Journal*, IBM has offered discounts of 10 percent to those who purchase by phone rather than from a traditional salesperson. What this tells the customer is that it benefits her to buy by phone because this medium offers savings that are passed along to her. It also makes competitors of the discounting firm seem to be padding expenses by not providing the same cost-cutting alternative to the customer.

Another approach to this situation is what Monsanto has done with one of its divisions. Because it was too costly to serve distant and marginal accounts with roadies, or traveling salespeople, Monsanto assigned a telerep to call accounts at the same time each month to service their needs. This has worked out very well because clients *know* that they are going to be in constant touch with the supplier and can plan their purchases accordingly.

Myth #7:   *The telephone is geared better to selling tangibles than intangibles.*

Those who endorse this myth are really reflecting insecurity about the merchandisability of their service or product through any medium. Over the telephone or in person, salespeople need to do essentially the same thing—sell *benefits*. If we haven't done our homework in identifying the most pertinent benefits for a prospect, we will be shut down through either presentational avenue. At the same time, if we have a clear conception of what the customer will gain by purchasing, and we communicate this notion clearly, we should arouse consent, irrespective of the medium employed. There is also an argument to be made for preferring the phone in selling intangibles. Because there are no distracting or competing visual cues provided by the presence of a salesperson or obtrusive sales aids, customers may be *more inclined to persuade themselves* because they can allow their imagination to work on behalf of accepting the offer.

The same kind of thinking supports direct mail marketers who elect not to place a photograph of a product or provider of a service into a mailing piece. The idea is that the absence of a photo will be less offensive than its presence. I recall trying to do business with an insurance salesman who insisted on making his pitch to me in person, presumably to answer my questions. I refused, noting that he could just as well quote a rate by phone or mail and save us time. He probably felt that he couldn't "control the prospect" by simply giving the requested quote through the most effective medium for the client. As a result, he balked and blew the deal.

As will be noted in our discussion of the Anatomy of a Sales Call in Chapter Four, the same sequence of persuasion is called for when selling either tangibles or intangibles.

Myth #8:   *It is easier for a prospect to say no to us on the phone.*

In some cases, this may be true. I know a pharmaceutical salesman who is a millionaire, having made his fortune as a roadie. By his own account, his success was attributable to "how I intimidate clients into buying." You see, he is about six foot nine, and weighs approximately two hundred and sixty-five pounds. When he leans over a doctor, a certain amount of pressure is placed upon the physician to buy or explain why he or she didn't. Most find it *easier* to buy when this fellow makes *his* rounds.

There is a degree of interpersonal pressure placed upon a prospect when he or she is looking at a salesperson and is about to say no. Nevertheless, this shouldn't be overestimated in its everyday impact. If we are savvy on the telephone, we can control the conversation so it becomes very unusual for a client to fail to hear us out or to hang up on us without having listened to our message. When we speak about handling resistance and objections in Chapter Five, we will provide tools for controlling the telephonic sales situation. Also, if we cultivate our ability to project our personalities over the phone, we should automatically discourage rejection of our message, while cementing commitment to ourselves as communicators.

Myth #9: *The telephone is an interruption that causes resentment.*

Whenever we are selling something, we have to first get someone's attention. This involves interrupting the activity in which the person had been engaged. It is unavoidable. Unfortunately, in thinking that she is interrupting the activity of a prospect in a negative way, the telephone marketer tends to make her own attitude negative, which causes the prospect to reject her message. In other words, if we think we are interrupting someone, we will communicate that concern to the person, and the person will act accordingly. If we act as if we are providing a valuable service that the prospect will naturally wish to hear, we are more likely to be received graciously. If you or your associates are involved in face-to-face selling, note what happens the next time you are sitting in the prospect's office in the middle of a sales pitch when the phone rings. Guess which conversation receives higher priority, yours or the caller's? You'll almost invariably find that *the phone call receives preference because it is fleeting,* while your presence is assured. We may exploit the preference shown to phone callers by first convincing ourselves that we will be speaking to someone who will be pleased that we interrupted him with a useful offer.

Myth #10: *Big deals can't be closed on the phone.*

Some folks believe the telephone is useful for moving minor products or services but is ill-suited for selling in more significant quantities. I know a fellow who disputed this belief and set forth to sell some very expensive "pink elephant" audiotape recording equipment by telephone. Others in his office thought he was foolish not to pound the pavement and see prospects face-to-face. The salesman figured that to move the equipment would involve the equivalent of finding the proverbial needle in a haystack. To move through as many prospects as quickly as possible, he chose a business directory of those people most likely to need the equipment. After one week, he told me he had sold $250,000 worth of product, earning himself about 10 percent of this substantial sum as a commission. If he had listened to associates, he might still be on the streets as you read this page!

I would argue that it is easier, in some cases, to sell big ticket items by phone for a few reasons. First, statistically fewer people are *qualified* to make such expenditures, and a large proportion of our calling will be geared to screening out the true prospects from the "suspects." Secondly, when we make an ornate ceremony out of selling a large amount of product, we tend to cause the buyer to be reluctant to make a commitment. By using the phone, we can effect a close in a very casual manner, without bringing inordinate attention to the gravity of the decision being made.

These are some of the myths that stand in the way of being successful in marketing by telephone. By systematically challenging the accuracy of these sorts of fictions we will be better able to clear a path to being maximally effective on the phone. In addition to the myths, we need to be aware of other psychological obstacles that we will encounter in telemarketing.

OUR BIGGEST FEARS: FAILURE, REJECTION, AND EVEN SUCCESS

Most of us have been raised by our parents and schoolteachers to avoid *failure* at all costs. When I attended school in Illinois, Michigan, and California, there was one thing that was the same in all grading schemes— the F grade that stood for failure. To receive an F was to be cursed with a terrible stigma. Most of us resolved to avoid this disgrace at all costs.

Unfortunately, what this tended to do to most of us was to encourage us to *avoid risks entirely*, for fear that we might be wrong and fail. As a result, many of us bring this profound fear with us to selling situations that we encounter. Still fearing failure, we avoid the risks associated with losing sales. In brief, we avoid the telephone because we are going to find the failure that we have been dodging for so many years.

Failure, however, has been given a bad name. Failure, as many psychologists and writers tell us, is often a very necessary prelude to success, and is a phenomenon that we are destined to live with as long as we occupy this human domain. In fact, failure can be the best thing for us, as I was informed by some very astute U.S. Navy scientists a few years ago.

I was privileged to participate in the largest civilian U.S. Navy project in history. One of the tasks I faced was to help senior-level Navy scientists to establish performance objectives by which to judge their success on the job. This was pretty tough for people who were busy trying to invent antigravity! In any case, a number of these people pointed out that it was difficult to determine when they were successful if we used conventional thinking. For instance, the scientists performed a number of experiments, many of which failed by one definition. In other words, they did not find the precise relationships they were searching for, and had to keep searching. Many of us would classify the experiments as failures, but the scientists correctly pointed out that this would be misleading. They noted that whenever they seemingly failed, they were moving closer to succeeding by eliminating certain discredited relationships in the subjects they were exploring. By sharing these failures with their colleagues instead of covering them up, the scientists were telling each other where *not* to look for certain answers to questions. In one sense, *continuous and controlled failures produced ultimate success.*

Many educators have come to see that failure is absolutely essential to the learning process. Unless we continuously take risks, we will not learn. Psychologists point out that we should welcome failure rather than abhor it, and that life itself is a process during which we must all experiment to determine what paths are worth pursuing at a given time.

Abraham Lincoln is a classical example of the merits of failing. Before he was elected to the Presidency, he lost every election in which he participated. Undaunted, he learned from each setback and ultimately earned the greatest post in the land.

We *will* fail on the telephone. As a matter of fact, we will probably fail to sell in 70–80 percent of our encounters. By accepting these setbacks as normal and by learning from them, we will become more and more capable.

FEAR OF REJECTION

Associated with our fear of failure is the fear of *rejection*. We incorrectly tell ourselves that in rejecting our sales message, prospects are rejecting *us*. We end up "self-downing," or telling ourselves things like, "Gary, you should be ashamed of yourself, you sounded so terrible on that call and may have offended the person." This kind of self-denigration is wasteful because it encourages us to dwell upon unsuccessful calls rather than make new ones where the chance of success resides.

I believe that beneath this fear of rejection is an unreasonable demand placed upon a number of us by our parents. "Be popular, and make people like you," we were told. "If somebody doesn't like you, it is your fault. Find out why, and change yourself in order to *make the person like you*." There are several false assumptions in these parental commands. One is that we can *make* someone like us. This is not possible. Statistically speaking, out of every hundred people we meet, a certain number simply will not like us at all. They may be envious, or they may associate us with one of their pet peeves, or they may hate people with red hair. No matter what we do to ourselves, we won't *make them* like us, and we'll probably end up disliking ourselves for the changes we are putting ourselves through for them. The assumption also exists in the parental edict that the highest value in life is being liked by everyone, and that we should do everything in our power to seek the approval of others. This kind of thinking tends to make us unduly timid and other-oriented instead of being self-directing, independent, and inner-oriented.

Telephone marketers *are* rejected more often than face-to-face salespeople for a very simple reason. *They make more calls*. With more calls, they stand a greater chance of hearing no than yes. We need to remember that rejection is routine and not exceptional. In fact, if we are going to receive no's 80 percent of the time, we should mentally check off the rejections we receive, noting that we are getting statistically closer and closer to an ultimate yes as we move along. In other words, if it takes ten calls to get a sale, and each sale is worth $100 to us, we make an average of $10 on each call whether that person has bought or not.

As we hear people tell us no, we should avoid saying to ourselves that we were awful, which is clearly not the case. Instead, think that the prospect missed out on the glorious opportunity of doing business with your firm and go on to the next call! The sooner we make the next call the better off we will be because we will not be stewing over our defeat.

FEAR OF SUCCESS

Believe it or not, a number of people suffer from the fear of being successful. Why is this so? Well, if they make a fantastic number of sales in a particular period, then everyone will come to expect higher performance from them in the future. The pressure will be horrendous, they think, and they will sooner or later come up short, and will be embarrassed by failure. So, in a certain sense, *the fear of success is really a fear of future failure*. Instead of performing up to one's potential, this person saves himself future pain by eliminating a present gain.

We need to remember that we *are not perfect*! We cannot be, and we don't have to be. So what if we are unable to maintain a certain number of sales from one period to the next? It may be unpleasant, but it isn't awful. Few things are, unless we tell ourselves they are. The best way to overcome the fear of failure, rejection, and success is to be self-accepting. No matter how we perform in a given context, we will still be okay. We are not only as good as our last sales presentation. We don't judge the ultimate value of professionals by any particular performance, but in how they perform, on the average, day in and day out, from one period to the next. The salesperson should be reminded that even the great Babe Ruth held another record besides most home runs. He had the distinction of being the strike-out king, who had more strike-outs registered against him than any other player. In short, he was the biggest success and the biggest failure at the same time! To achieve significant results, we need to respect the fact that these two outcomes do go hand-in-hand.

GET OFF THE SELF-ESTEEM ROLLER COASTER

Most of us are interested in improving our sales performance, and one means for doing this is to analyze our past performances. For instance, if we are finishing an unsuccessful call, our first tendency is to ask ourselves, "What went wrong on that one?" The problem with this sort of "instant replay" is that we interrupt our calling cycle and tend to focus our criticism in the wrong place.

If we get the order, we tell ourselves, "I'm great," and if we lose it, "I'm lousy." These extremes of self-judgment tend to place us on what I call the "self-esteem roller coaster." One moment, we are on top of the world, and the next, we're in the pits. This is one of the processes that occurs when we get "pumped up" by a positive-attitude philosophy that encourages us to tell ourselves we are great or perfect. Inevitably, we will face a customer who will dispute this, and we will become emotionally deflated and perhaps depressed, which will obviously not help our sales effort.

Instead of riding the self-esteem roller coaster, we should focus our self-criticism upon our behaviors and not our inherent goodness or badness. By doing so, we can objectively change the impediments to selling, while identifying and refining our own personal success formula.

DON'T JOIN
THE PROCRASTINATORS' CLUB

I understand there is a procrastinators' club that struggles to have a meeting once a year. Unfortunately, they never seem to get around to deciding when and where to have it! On the serious side, procrastination is an occupational problem that faces many of us. Why do we procrastinate? What can we do about it?

Procrastination is simply delaying some action until some time in the future, and the delay may cause us some sort of loss. We may lose the quality job that would result from doing something right away. We may cause ourselves psychological pain by knowing that we should get something done and punishing ourselves with self-downing when we observe ourselves not doing it. We may also serve to hang up other people who are depending upon our swift actions.

Procrastination is a negative habit pattern that can be caused by an acute fear of failure. Instead of facing the prospect of failing based on the merits of our performance, we instead delay acting, and attribute any failure we experience to the "little time" that we had to complete the task. We can look at someone else and say, "What do you expect from somebody who had to put the thing together in twenty minutes?" Poor time management leads to procrastination as well. If we fail to set priorities and act upon them, we will find that we are getting behind. After we are behind, we may procrastinate to avoid the failure that we will encounter by not getting certain tasks done. Some of us become procrastinators because we tend to avoid the hard work that will be required to perform a difficult task well.

One of the great problems telephone marketing reps will experience is procrastination. If they are working in a central office where there is supervision, they will probably avoid making that first telephone call, for fear that it will be a rejection. What reps will do is have two or three cups of coffee and gossip with their peers before they gingerly make that first sales call. You may find that reps tend to spend too much time between calls because they fear rejection.

If you are going to make calls from home, or your salespeople are, procrastination will be of greater significance because it is easy to give in to the inevitable distractions that occur in our habitats. One of the ways to overcome the problem is to insist that a certain number of contacts be made each and every hour. Additionally, a "bits and pieces" approach can work, whereby a rep begins his calling shift by making easy callbacks first, followed by more difficult cold calls. I used to tell myself that I wouldn't allow myself to get up from my desk to get a cup of coffee until I had gotten at least two orders. If this meant that I would be sitting in the chair for twenty minutes or two hours, it didn't matter. What I was doing was contracting with myself to give myself a reward if I started the task right away and was successful with it, and I would not reward myself if unsuccessful.

I find it helpful to remind myself that "I'm not going to be perfect" before I get on the phone. This makes me relax. I recognize that I can and will make mistakes, and that it's all right. This makes calling a lot more fun, and easier to get into doing right away.

AVOID THE COSTLY SECONDARY GAIN TRAP

Most of us go to work for at least a few reasons. We hope to gain certain things. Some of these things may be classified as primary gains, such as a healthy paycheck, good benefits, and, perhaps, job security. Additionally, we may enjoy our jobs because they provide such secondary gains as comraderie with co-workers, a chance to meet interesting people from different walks of life, and a chance to belong to a certain type of company or industry.

All of these goals are normal and probably desirable. What tends to happen to salespeople, though, is that they unconsciously start putting *secondary* gains ahead of *primary* gains. Here's how it works. We all want to make money, if we are salespeople. At the same time, we all have a certain need to be liked by others. Sometimes we allow our need to be liked to get in the way of our efforts to make money. I remember doing a telephone sales seminar in Amarillo, Texas a few years ago. One fellow in the program sold insurance and said, "I refuse to sell anyone an insurance policy until they are my friend, first." I inquired about what someone needed to do to qualify as a friend, and he replied, "Well, I have to feel that we can talk about other things besides insurance, and that we could just sit down and have a cup of coffee together." What this fellow was doing was putting his idea of friendship ahead of the primary goal, which was getting sales.

Telephone reps may put being accepted or being liked or even not being rejected ahead of making strong sales appeals to prospects. You may also find yourself or others yielding to the request by prospects for literature or brochures instead of closing the person then and there on the phone. These would be added examples of falling into the secondary gain trap.

What we need to do is systematically ask ourselves whether we are accepting secondary gains where we should be looking for primary ones. I know very good salespeople who lose sale after sale because they feel they have to prove they are smarter than the prospects they are trying to sell. They are putting their concept of smartness ahead of getting orders.

BUILD YOUR FRUSTRATION TOLERANCE

Many of us suffer from something called "low frustration tolerance." What this means is that we seek instant gratification of all of our needs, and when we are frustrated in having any needs satisfied, we reject the activity that will eventually give us satisfaction.

New telemarketers have this problem. They, like most of us, want sales right away. When sales aren't immediately forthcoming, they get frustrated. Instead of putting up with the frustration, reps give up on the job and decide, "this isn't for me." What they may do is go down the street to the next place of employment and say the same thing when they encounter barriers to success.

Telephone reps need to appreciate that they may have to make a hundred or more presentations before they get their first order. The odds in telephone selling are different than on the streets. If we are making face-to-face sales appeals, we may close one out of every four people with whom we speak. On the phone our success rate may be lower. We'll do better if we thicken our skins to the negative feedback we get until we start getting some of the positive results that will occur over time.

GO FOR THE GUSTO
ON EACH AND EVERY CALL!

When I used to play baseball I would solicit the opinions of athletic trainers to discover the best methods of preparing myself for the sport. They told me that they could make me stronger through a weight-training program, and they might be able to increase my stamina through running. Each trainer pointed out, though, that if I wanted to improve my *baseball* skills, I'd have to play that sport as often as I could, while driving myself to my limits each time. The same reasoning applies to doing well on the telephone. The best "exercise" is to make calls and try to get as much accomplished from every call as possible. This means that we should try to close or receive some sort of commitment with each contact. Naturally, we will be rebuffed frequently. Nonetheless, by "going for the gusto" on each and every call we will increase our ability to realize benefits each time. We should tell ourselves that each call must come to a preordained conclusion. If this means that it will take three calls to accomplish our ultimate agreement, each call must do its part in achieving that outcome.

SET GOALS AND RESOLVE
TO DO BETTER AND BETTER

There is an old expression that says that if we fail to identify goals for our-selves, we will be sure to reach them. In other words, no matter what our level of performance is, we will be inclined to accept it and strive no further. Goals are terribly important if we want to achieve success. I like to identify the number and quality of sales I expect to make before every work shift. As I move from one call to the next, I may place visual reminders in front of me that tell me that I have "ten more sales to go," and so forth. What this does is keep my attention riveted upon the outcome I wish to produce.

I once heard a wise person claim that the greatest tragedy in life is reaching our goals and getting what we always wanted. What is meant here is that we need to continually revise our targets upward, lest we find we arrive at a certain level and become complacent. Without a continuing struggle toward goals, our lives may become meaningless. I like to challenge my own limitations by examining the things I tell myself about what is and is not possible to produce. For instance, I have told myself that most deals will be for x number of dollars, because they seem to have fallen into this range in the past. There is no divine decree that this *must* be the case in the future. What I am doing is limiting my sights to what is *probable* without accepting the challenge of what is *possible*. Constant updating of our performance objectives is needed to produce maximal achievement.

REMEMBER THE LAW OF LARGE NUMBERS

Statistical probability is on the side of telemarketers. We have noted some of the problems associated with making a large number of calls, including the fact that we will receive a large proportion of rejections. This is true. At the same time, though, we are increasing our odds of hearing a yes.

I have always marveled at representatives of firms that have recently broken into telemarketing and think they have "invented the wheel." Their first response to telemarketing is elation because they are closing as much or more business as they used to in the field, yet they are lowering their costs dramatically. What they fail to see is that they have experienced a windfall largely because the law of large numbers is now working for them, where it couldn't operate efficiently in the field.

Their next challenge, of course, is to improve and systematize the telemarketing function, though if they simply continue to use a home-made program, they will probably do better than they had been doing because they will be bailed out by statistical probability. In simple terms, "keep throwing stuff against the wall, and some of it's bound to stick."

AVOID CALL CONTAMINATION

It is easy to let one call contaminate future calls if the first was a real "bummer" or "downer." What we end up doing after we hang up on a bad call is carry over the ill tone of that call into the next, which is a natural reaction. Of course, the recipient of our next presentation has no idea of what transpired on previous calls, and she only hears a down in the mouth salesperson on her end, to whom she is inclined to respond negatively.

What can we do to prevent call contamination? I urge you to take *one deep breath* between each call you place or take, irrespective of the mood of the prior call. This will help you to feel composed and in control. You will sound positive and in charge of the situation to the next party which will help your sales.

Breathing is at the core of many philosophies of self-control, includ-ing various forms of yoga and meditation. It has such a restorative quality that it is recommended for use in treating acute stress reactions. I have heard psychologists recommend we take four deep breaths after stressful encounters. Don't do this between calls, though. It will make you high!

TRY TO LEAVE ALL CALLS
ON A POSITIVE NOTE

Occasionally we speak to people who are bitter toward us for one reason or other. By the time we are about to say goodbye, they are sounding particularly caustic. I suggest we avoid giving in to their negativity by leav-ing the call on the highest plane possible. End such calls with the phrase, "Thank you for your courtesy." As you can tell, it's very important to say these words *without sarcasm*. If we have *any* edge in our voices, we will make the person feel terrible, which is not our intention.

What does this accomplish for us? We can take satisfaction in the idea that *we have taken control of the call back into our own hands* by ending the call pleasantly. Moreover, the prospect will usually be impressed with our maturity and composure, and his or her regard for our company will be improved. Most importantly, the other person will be much more likely to buy from us the next time we call.

BE GOOD TO YOU!

When you accomplish something, compliment yourself, no matter how insignificant the telephonic victory was. For instance, you might be getting further and further along in your presentation before having the call terminated by prospects. This could be a source of self-derision, but it needn't be. See it as a positive trend, and get on cheerfully with the next call.

PSYCH UP YOUR FELLOW SALESPEOPLE

I find this practice helpful if I am calling or supervising others who are selling. When one rep takes the time to encourage another, it is often time well spent, because it produces a cooperative climate throughout the sales room. It is also very smart for one person to be the "buddy" of another, because in praising or helping the other person we are assuring that we will receive the same sort of positive treatment in the future.

EXPECT SUCCESS
ON EVERY CALL

Many of us have heard of self-fulfilling prophecy, which suggests that we will make something come true if we believe it strongly enough. This happens quite a bit on the phone. If we sound negative while telling ourselves, "I'll never get this order," we are likely to fail. At the same time, if we say to ourselves before each call, "I'm going to get this one," we are more likely to succeed than fail.

WORK YOUR WAY OUT
OF A NEGATIVE MOOD

From time to time, sales reps have legitimate excuses to avoid selling. Someone in the immediate family may have passed away, or they are fighting a fierce bout of the flu. These are usually justifiable reasons for missing some telephone selling time.

Sometimes, however, we will make an excuse out of something a little less meaningful. We might say, "I can't bring myself to sell today because my second cousin's hamster just died, and I'm overwrought." In a situation such as this, I suggest the sales rep *try to sell* for just a few minutes, and if he or she still feels depressed, an excuse for the rest of the shift will be granted.

It is amazing to witness the power of constructive work to help people forget their woes. Before long, they find they are getting sales and feeling better about their circumstances and themselves.

BEWARE OF THE SEVEN FALSE BELIEFS

At the root of our psychological resistance toward selling by telephone may lie one of seven false beliefs about other people and our performance. Whenever we hear ourselves repeating these notions, we should challenge their truthfulness:

1. *I need to be liked by every single prospect in order to be successful.* As we recall from the discussion of the secondary gain trap, this notion is incorrect. It certainly helps to have the goodwill of others, but there are certain folks who simply won't like us or our message. We aren't perfect, and we can't be perfectly popular, either. As long as we develop a successful sales routine and repeat it enough, we will be successful.

2. *I have to be a complete winner in each selling situation to consider myself worthwhile.* This places an unnecessary burden of perfection on our shoulders. It is also mathematically incorrect. If we have to get the approval of each and every prospect to be successful, we aren't speaking with enough people, or we're in the wrong business.

3. *I have other people to blame for my lack of performance.* Clearly,

we should acknowledge that we are the captains of our own ships and stop blaming the environment, or our calling lists, or our managers for our lack of achievement.

4. *It is the end of the world when I don't get that big sale.* It is normal to build up our hopes that we will get a large sale, especially when we have been working toward that end for some time. We should avoid putting all our emotional eggs in one basket by working on a large number of prospects simultaneously. If one or two fall through, we won't then be devastated.

5. *Other people are sure making me unhappy!* It's true that others are capable of doing some pretty unpleasant things. No one, however, should be given the power to *make us happy or unhappy.* We should remember that we *choose* to feel happy or unhappy, and we have the power to alter our own moods while preventing others from doing this to us.

6. *It is easier to delay hearing what might be a rejection from a prospect than to face it squarely.* Sometimes we just feel that a prospect we have been cultivating is going to tell us no if we call to receive his or her verdict on the matter. Instead of calling, as we should, we avoid hearing the bottom line. I have found it much more satisfactory to hear bad news quickly. In fact, it may be advisable to call prospects from whom you are expecting a decision a day or two *early* to help expedite the process. I recall promising to get back to a prospect after he requested a two week period to think things over. I waited to the exact day, only to be told when I called that a competitor was given the business two days earlier for no reason other than the fact that he happened upon the prospect at the right time. It's better to be a little early than too late.

7. *Just because I have sold with a certain style in the past means I must continue using that same style in the future. In other words, I can't change!* This is baloney because we can and do change, no matter what we think about it. We can always improve our selling approach. If we stop growing and experimenting we fall behind the competition.

In speaking with a telephone pro the other day, a man who has been in telemarketing for twenty years, I heard a significant insight about the process. He said the "toughest things about this business isn't the customer; it's the sales reps themselves." He elaborated on how difficult it is to find reps who can maintain a positive attitude about their jobs while routinely performing at full tilt.

The key to success is in understanding ourselves and our psychological responses to the demands of telemarketing. When we are aware of the common traps we are heir to, we can go about the systematic job of overcoming each obstacle as it appears before us.

Perhaps more than other arenas, telemarketing demands that we bring ourselves under control in order to realize the full benefits that this medium has to offer.

chapter three

The sixty
telemarketing canons

A major complaint one hears from organizations these days is that phone costs are soaring through the roof with no end in sight. In some firms, "call abuse" is the concern, where employees are using company resources to call friends and loved ones in distant towns. For the most part, though, the main culprit is something more subtle and widespread. People simply are unprepared to efficiently manage their business affairs when they get on the phone. They don't have a very clear idea of their goals for particular calls, nor the means to be employed to reach those goals.

This chapter is devoted my telephone marketing "canons," or the sixty rules I have developed for how we should prepare ourselves and our materials before and as we do our telemarketing. I will warn you in advance that some of these principles may appear to be foreign to your accustomed habits. This is only natural, because if you didn't hear anything new from me, I wouldn't be providing you with a real service. What I ask is that you not only read these items, but later "try them on," so to speak, in your everyday telephone rituals to determine their effectiveness for you.

The canons are really twelve broad types of suggestions broken down further into five smaller units each, for a total of sixty tips in all. These ideas will appear to you as what you should *know, have* at hand, *think, do,* and *not do* as you start your calling. They should provide you with an idea of the physical and mental tools you will need to be maximally effective on the phone.

A summary of the canons appears in the grid like configuration at the end of this chapter for easy reference and recall.

Canon #1: *Know thy prospects*

I have worked in telemarketing rooms where management provided several walls filled with shelves containing Yellow Page directories for various cities in the United States. What we were asked to do, as reps, was decide each morning who we were going to call. At least, the more organized reps did this. Everyone else decided who to contact as they moved from one call to the next, instead of having a large list of intended callees in front of them.

What this did was make reps spend much too much time between calls making decisions. They had to do their actual marketing work as they moved along trying to sell certain categories of business. Typically, reps would waste as much as 70 percent of their productive potential musing over whether to call Al's Auto Repair or Betty's House of Beauty next.

The first canon, therefore, is that we *should know who our prospects are before we begin our calling.*

Canon #2: *Have your materials in front of you*

When we have determined who we are going to call, it should be a relatively easy matter to have our calling lists in front of us where they can be easily accessed. At the same time, we should have plenty of other tools, such as pens, order forms, and especially our calendars. There may be no embarrassment as stinging as having to ask a buyer to "hold on while I look for my calendar," particularly if the other party is planning on booking a delivery of product with you.

Where can we get calling lists? Well, I suggest we use some of the free sources available to us whenever we can. Such lists include the yellow pages, published by local phone companies as well as private publishers, existing customer lists, including inactive accounts, which may be very profitable if approached correctly. You will also want to befriend the people in the directories or reference section of your largest local public library. I know that the Los Angeles Public Library, downtown branch, has some very highly skilled research people who can advise one about the types of directories that may be available given certain marketing objectives. Although the directories may not be removed from the library, we may certainly copy the names of persons and firms contained therein, as well as determine if we should purchase the directory for intensive use. You'd be amazed at the number of directories available. In fact, I suggest you look into Bernard Klein's classic compendium, *Guide to American Directories*, which may be found in the reference sections of many public libraries.

If you want to contact a very narrowly targeted group, you will probably wish to call a "list broker," who can be found in your telephone book. The broker is a person who assembles and rents names which may be contacted by mail or provides phone numbers for the purpose of telemarketing. He or she will be able to obtain particular lists of, say, subscribers to *Time* magazine, or even compile a blend of names from various sources. Typical fees run in the range of $35 to $95 per thousand names, including the broker's fee, if the names are delivered on mailing labels. If you wish the information, including phone number, to appear on cards, the cost is usually in the range of five to ten times the cost of labels because of the added computer time involved in transferring the data to a special medium.

Trade and professional associations are excellent sources of prospects. You may wish to join certain organizations as an associate or auxiliary member, which can enable you to receive the group's membership roster. Some associations sell the names of their members as a matter of course. If you think your market may be captured in a trade group or association, I suggest you look into a directory called *National Trade and Professional Associations of the United States and Canada and Labor Unions*, published annually (Washington, D.C. · Columbia Books, Inc.). This will provide you with the names of most associations with national membership.

You may always use your imagination to drum up a unique and effective list for yourself. Let's say you are in the tuxedo and formalwear business, and you want to rent suits and gowns for special occasions. You might obtain a list of college and high school seniors in the area. You could also call local florists to see if they have a list of weddings and other events that they intend to service, and instead of renting their list, you might agree to exchange a certain number of names from your own customer list.

Canon #3: *Make a mental checklist of the tools you will need.*

You should be telling yourself, "I need to prepare my tools in order to be successful. What do I need to do next?" By staying on top of your organizational needs you will avoid costly down-time and delays in moving swiftly from one prospect to the next.

Canon #4: *Presort all prospects the night or day before calling.*

If you intend to make calling priorities and rate the desirability of calling certain prospects in a given sequence, this work should be performed before sitting down to do one's calling. As you may have gathered, I am a strong believer in the power of concentrating on one thing at a time as we are selling. Any distractions will cause us to lose effectiveness.

Canon #5: *Do not pluck prospects out of thin air*

One of the most time-consuming habits we can fall into is inventing a calling list as we go along, by thinking, "Maybe I'll call Acme Plumbing next; no, perhaps Al's Burgers. I just passed by there on the way to work this morning." Call every name on your list, and avoid deviating from your plan.

Canon #6: *Know 95 percent of what you are going to say during the call.*

Most telemarketers encounter their greatest problem in not feeling comfortable with their presentations. On one call, they might sound great, and on the next, terrible. Some days they may feel so miserable that each sales talk sounds uninspired and rather pathetic. The words just don't seem to be flowing right.

This problem may be eliminated by *deciding in advance what we are going to say on each call.* This does mean that calls will be highly rehearsed and somewhat uniform in content.

Canon #7: *Have a typed, thorough presentation in front of you at all times.*

This is a very practical suggestion for a number of reasons. First, we need to know where we are *headed* at all times during a sales talk. By having a script in front of us, we have clarity in terms of our objective for a call and the path that will be used to reach it. If we lose our place as we are selling, it is a simple thing to gracefully recover our poise and momentum by referring back to the presentation.

In having a written talk we will be making our appeals as scientific as they can be as long as a live person is delivering them. Only through repeating a winning formula can we hope to reap maximum rewards.

Canon #8: *Each talk we give needs to sound fresh and spontaneous.*

You might be asking how a talk can sound spontaneous when it is scripted in advance, or "canned." Well, think about show business for a minute. One of my favorite musicals is *A Chorus Line.* I enjoy watching the cast dance and move from one scene to the next. I have seen a number of productions of the play, yet they are all carbon copies of each other. Literally, *nothing changes from one performance to the next.* As audiences, how do we respond to this sort of canned approach. We love it. In fact, if the musical changed from one performance to the next in radical ways, we would probably call the resulting efforts "unprofessional." Indeed, a significant measure of the professionalism of the cast is that they are disciplined enough to set forth a performative plan and follow it to the letter, night after night.

We need to be able to do the same sort of thing to be as successful and professional as we can be as telemarketers. As one very successful businessman puts it, "Maybe it's not as exciting to keep doing the same thing again and again and again—even though it's the most profitable."

Canon #9: *Follow the presentation on a word-for-word basis.*

This is what I affectionately refer to as my "Lockstep Monster." The main reason it is so important to keep to a written presentation is that it is the most efficient way of getting a sale. When we start to hem and haw, we lose the power we need to build the appeal for the customer. Moreover, we will probably start introducing "devil terms" into the talk that will sap the strength of the appeal.

When we have an established script or patterned sales talk, we can better measure slight changes that we introduce from time to time. If more than one aspect of a talk changes, it is much more difficult to determine what is causing the results we are getting.

Canon #10: *Don't deviate from the planned talk because you think the prospect will be bored by it.*

It is a common mistake to project our own sense of boredom upon an unsuspecting prospect. Because *we* have uttered something a few hundred times, we naturally tend to believe that the next person will find the talk boring, although she has never heard it before!

If you are growing stale on a sales talk, change it in *constructive ways,* one item at a time. In this manner, you will build upon your success.

Canon #11: *Remember that the law of large numbers pays off for telemarketers.*

As we noted in Chapter Two, the law of large numbers tells us that we will be successful if we call enough people, because, statistically speaking, some of them will have to say yes. This should be comforting to us, especially when we hear no several times in a row.

Canon #12:   *Have at least twenty prospect cards in front of you for each intended hour of calling.*

To fully take advantage of the statistical possibilities in telemarketing, we should never allow ourselves to run out of people to call. If you are engaged in a mass marketing effort, where you are trying to reach as many people as possible, you will probably wish to make your presentation last no more than two minutes. If so, depending upon the types of people you are trying to reach, you may move through as many as twenty lead cards per hour or more. Have at least this number on hand.

You have no doubt noted that I mention having lead *cards*. I favor using 4" x 6" index cards for storing basic information about prospects. In this way, your desk will be orderly, and you will be able to write keyword notes on the cards to indicate that a call-back should be made or that the person will be available for a call at some later date. Cards will also be handy to set aside into different piles to provide for future filing or re-calling.

You may find that list brokers hesitate to make available the size of card set forth here. It's true that their standard size is 3" x 5", but I find there is little space left over for my notes with such cards. Be insistent. If they wish to, they can have the computers generate data on the cards you need.

Canon #13:   *You should be thinking, "Each call I make is paying off for me."*

Is this the case if you are rejected? Sure. Let's say that it takes you ten calls to make a sale, and that a sale will be worth one hundred dollars. Well, as you hear the ninth person in a row decline, you might tell yourself that you have made no money to that point. Technically, you are correct, but *statistically* speaking, you have made $90. All it takes is for you to make the next presentation in order to receive the entire commission, or $100, for an average of $10 per contact.

I find this sort of thinking much more pleasant than some negative alternatives, because it makes us thicker skinned and much more willing to go on and make the next attempt to sell.

Canon #14:   *Move through your call cards in an orderly fashion.*

No matter what priority you have assigned to calling your prospects, try to follow it. This contributes to time management and peace of mind.

Canon #15:   *Don't skip around your calling cards, thinking that this will make you lucky.*

I am amazed at the number of people who are superstitious about various elements of their selling procedures. Some show their feelings in this regard by skipping over certain cards because they "don't like the names" of the companies. This is absurd. Let's say there are two banks listed in a directory, "Serious Bank and Trust," and "Happy State Bank." Well, I suppose I would be inclined to call the latter because I can easily imagine that the folks there will be easier to sell. This is probably wrong for a few reasons. First, I assure you that "Happy State Bank" receives *disproportionately more calls* because of its name. Having to deal with that many sales messages makes the folks there pretty resistant to persuasion, while "Serious Bank and Trust" sounds so off-putting that the people there are seldom approached to buy anything. Secondly, because "Happy State Bank" is listed alphabetically before "Serious Bank and Trust," it is called more frequently by sales people who begin to call a list and give up before they reach the end of the category. In a sense, we may also persuade ourselves that one person will or will not be receptive, and *actually cause the outcome we have anticipated.*

Canon #16:   *You should know that you are in charge of your own feelings about selling.*

Avoid tellling yourself untruths, such as, "Well, it's just not my day." Does some powerful force outside you determine that today, Tuesday, is not going to be Harry Jones' day, nor Gary Goodman's? I don't think so. Each day is as potentially fruitful as the next.

Canon #17:   *Place inspirational items around your work area to motivate you.*

I think it is important for us to be able to personalize our surroundings to help us feel comfortable. I like to post pictures of material items that I am working toward having one day, such as certain kinds of cars, homes, and the like. Some folks like to place photos of their families before them, as reminders of why they are working so diligently.

Canon #18:   *Tell yourself, "On every call, I'm getting better and better."*

This phrase is borrowed from a self-help psychologist who, around the turn of the century, used to have his patients tell themselves, "Every day, in every way, I'm getting better and better." He found that repeating this phrase helped people to heal themselves and build their self-esteem. In moving from one call to the next, if we tell ourselves we are continuously improving, we will sound more positive all the time and be more successful as a result.

Canon #19:   *Try to take responsibility for your own attitude at any given moment.*

It is easy to blame others for our lack of performance. When we're not selling, we look for excuses. All of a sudden, the voice of one of our associates may begin to grate on us, or we might blame the last client with whom we spoke for putting us in a bad mood. When you find you are telling yourself such negative things, stop yourself and challenge the validity of what you are saying. You will find that you feel better because you are taking charge of your own mood and attitude.

Canon #20:   *Avoid psyching yourself out with false beliefs.*

These ideas have been articulated in Chapter Two on the psychology of telemarketing, and include such self-statements and assertions as "every single prospect must like me for me to be successful in selling," and "I have to be perfect in all sales efforts to be successful."

Canon #21:   *Know as many product features as possible.*

It is important to have identifiable features of our products and services that may be verbally demonstrated to prospects on the phone. By using creativity, we can sometimes find hidden features that we didn't realize existed.

Canon #22:   *Have available a no-hands written guide to product features.*

It is extremely helpful to have a list of product features to which we may instantly refer at any time. Your no-hands guide may consist of a board system, such as the one at the end of this chapter.

Canon #23:   *Ask yourself what the most relevant product features may be for a particular type of prospect.*

Some salespeople waste the time of prospects by speaking about irrelevant product features. The prospect, in the meantime, is wondering, "Why is she talking about all of these things; they're of no concern to me." By determining which features are most relevant, we will make our listeners happy.

Canon #24:   *Limit the number of features you mention in your talk.*

People have the attention span of hamsters when they are listening to a phone sales presentation. Therefore, it is best to be as succinct as possible. Limit the number of product features you discuss to two to four.

Canon #25:   *Don't rely upon memory to recall important features that may need mentioning.*

Keep the features list right in front of you at all times, not obscured by other papers, coffee cups, and the like.

Canon #26:   *Know as many product benefits as possible.*

As you may be aware already, benefits differ from features in an important way: features tell a client what something is, while benefits tell the person what the product or service will *do* for them. The distinction is important because, typically, people decide to buy something based upon anticipated benefits, and not based on features alone. Many salespeople get this backwards, and insist on mentioning what something is without translating it into its payoff for the customer.

Canon #27:   *Have a no-hands written guide to benefits before you.*

As with features, benefits should always be visible to us.

Canon #28:   *Ask yourself what the most relevant product benefits are for a particular type of prospect.*

All customers do not respond to the same benefits of a particular product or service, though they may all be buyers for one reason or other.

Canon #29:   *Limit the number of benefits you mention in your talk.*

As with features, we should restrict the number of benefits we mention to two to four. The reason is that customers tend to disbelieve our claim if we contend that there are "101 reasons they should buy."

Canon #30: *Don't rely upon memory to recall important benefits that may require mentioning.*

When we come to the stage in the presentation known as the close, and the prospect says, "I'm not really interested," he is telling us that we have mentioned the wrong benefits, and that we should probe his needs and mention appropriate ones. To do so smoothly, we shouldn't try to remember obscure benefits under the pressure of the moment.

Canon #31: *We should have several ways to open a sales call smoothly.*

Knowing how we are going to begin calls is an indispensable comfort. By eliminating any fuzziness in the overture, we are more likely to create harmony at the end of calls.

Canon #32: *Have at hand a list of thirteen openers.*

When we discuss the anatomy of a sales call in Chapter Four, we will provide a list of thirteen types of openers that may be combined to produce hundreds of fresh ways to break the ice with prospects.

Canon #33: *Ask yourself, "Which opener will work best with this type of person?"*

Some prospects will respond very favorably to an "inactive account" approach, if they have once done business with us, instead of a "new service" approach. We should determine in advance how we are going to approach different clients.

Canon #34: *Use a planned opener on every call.*

While it may seem contrived to some of us, prospects really do respond better when they feel that the call is being efficiently handled from the beginning. That's why it is imperative to use a stylized opener that has been determined to get the call smoothly underway.

Canon #35:   *Don't wing it in the beginning of the call.*

We don't sound nearly as friendly or nice or open as we think we do when we try to be spontaneous in the beginning of a call. Instead, we usually just sound dumb. Sometimes the ritual at the beginning of a call can get too long, for example, when we are inquiring into the well-being of each and every family member of the prospect's household.

Canon #36:   *We should have several ways to close sales calls.*

It has been said by some that the close is the most crucial part of any sales transaction, because it is here that we are asking for the order in a strategic manner. I suggest three closes be employed: (1) The choice close; (2) the power-assumptive close; and (3) the assumptive-checkback close. These will be described in detail in the next chapter.

Canon #37:   *Have a list of good closing phrases before you.*

Because closing terminology is tricky, it is urgent that we always have our phrases within reach so they may be introduced into calls at the appropriate times. Sometimes we will want to use a number of closes within the same call and to do so requires immediate access to them.

Canon #38:   *Ask yourself, "Which close will work best with this type of prospect?"*

When you have analyzed the type of buyer you will be facing you can decide which sort of close would be appropriate with the person based upon the gentle force needed in the situation. For example, if you are only asking someone to try a product on a trial basis, it may be necessary to use very mild persuasion, and you can choose to use the assumptive-checkback close for this purpose. If you are asking for action that is substantial, as you might be by selling a very expensive item, you might elect to use either the choice close or the power-assumptive close, thus minimizing the amount of inner conflict experienced by the customer in making a decision to purchase. If you are dealing with a wishy-washy buyer, you may wish to use the power-assumptive close on an exclusive basis, because the customer is really asking you to make the decision for him or her.

Canon #39:   *Use a planned closer on every call.*

Selling can seem to be like the gunfight at the OK corral. The salesperson ambles down the road to meet the adversary, and just as the time approaches to draw and shoot, the hand is frozen in space and no shot is fired. This is what happens when we move our prospect through a sales sequence without bringing in a close at the right time. We lose the contest.

In recognizing that the real objective of every call is to effect some kind of favorable outcome or close, we will be preparing ourselves to close once, twice, or even three or four times if necessary, on each call. By practicing our craft we will definitely become better and better at it.

Canon #40:   *Never wait for a prospect to close.*

It is a sad fact that if we, as salespeople, fail to close, the prospect will seldom bail us out, unless the person is in desperate need of what we are selling. I know that some selling experts contend that silence is one of the most potent closing tools available to a salesperson. In face-to-face situations, where our physical presence may be intimidating, they may be right. On the phone, however, we will get eaten alive if we pause too long or in the wrong places. Therefore, bring each call to a close yourself, and then pick up the money that's lying on the table. You earned it.

Canon #41:   *We should know the steps involved in confirming sales.*

When we receive a yes at what seems to be the end of our sales talk, this can put us on top of the world. All we usually want to do at that moment is kiss our phone and congratulate ourselves on a job well done. It's too early to celebrate at that moment, however. We have a few more things to say and do before we leave the buyer.

When an agreement is consummated by phone, we should immediately review with the buyer the terms of the deal he or she assented to for the purpose of creating mutual clarity and removing any lingering misconceptions about particulars.

Let's say that we are trying to set up appointments for field sales reps to follow up and visit the following week. If we don't make a reminder call to the prospect a few days in advance of the visit, she may not be clear that we have produced a solid appointment. The way to reduce uncertainty, as well as cut down on missed appointments, is to confirm the details of the impending visit with the customer *while we are on the first call.*

Canon #42:   *We should have a written confirmation before us.*

As with any other vital part of our talk, the confirmation segment should be directly in front of us at all times. There are six segments to a good confirmation that are reviewed in the next chapter on the anatomy of a sales call. These segments clarify delivery details, check billing details, test the customer for her understanding of the transaction, allow for unanswered questions, congratulate the buyer on a wise decision, and attempt to leave the party feeling positive about the agreement.

Canon #43:   *We should be thinking that when we reach agreement, we need to test the strength of the understanding right away.*

This should be a matter of course as we sell. If you supervise other people, you will notice that they will want to skip the confirmation because sales will blow out there. Tell them that's one of the very purposes of the confirmation, to delete weak deals that should go no further.

Canon #44:   *We need to allow the prospect to express uncertainty, if it exists.*

Some customers possess such weak egos that they are unable to say no to us during sales calls. At first, we might wish this malady upon all of our customers, but, in fact, it is a problem. Such folks have buyers' remorse, and end up unwinding the deal anyway. And they usually back out at the worst time, after we have invested time, money, and other resources in trying to meet our part of the bargain. It's better to discard such poor orders in the beginning of the process rather than later. If a customer expresses misgivings during the confirmation, we should try to save the order by re-selling the benefits to be derived. If she insists, let her go, and move on to the next order.

By allowing customers to express misgivings, we are probably stengthening our otherwise solid sales because we are showing the customer that we are secure enough to allow the person to participate in the closing moments of the call and ask any questions she wishes to ask.

Canon #45: *Condition yourself to be graceful when the person says yes, and to smoothly control the call thereafter.*

It's easy to turn into mush when we think we have an order. When the person says yes to our offer, we should tell ourselves, "now the real selling begins." By the time we have completed the confirmation, we may be in a position to sweeten the deal by upselling the buyer, or by selling him an add-on item that is related in some way to the original purchase item.

Canon #46: *We should know effective ways to control the conversation by delaying objections.*

As will be discussed in detail in Chapter Five, there are times when we will *not want to answer objections* because doing so would keep us from closing properly. When we reach such a point in our sales talks we will use *transition phrases.*

Canon #47: *We should have several transition phrases before us.*

I will be giving you six transition phrases that may be used to delay objections when we discuss the subject in Chapter Five. It is helpful to have several because you will find calls in which you may need to use two or three in order to lead the call to a successful conclusion.

Canon #48:   *Tell yourself, "I will answer no objection before it's time."*

Just as Paul Masson will "drink no wine before it's time," neither should we prematurely answer an objection. If we attempt to answer an objection as it is raised, we may sound unduly argumentative and lose the sale.

Canon #49:   *Delay answering objections if they are raised before you reach your close.*

One of the ideas behind this suggestion is that most objections we hear before we have reached our first close are premature. People are really saying, "I don't *think* I'll be interested," before they have a chance to hear us out. What we do, in delaying the objection, is to gently persuade them to listen to the remainder of our message before coming to a decision.

Canon #50:   *We should never argue with a prospect.*

It is sometimes tempting to tell a prospect he or she is flat-out wrong, especially when the person makes an inane objection. We need to bite our tongues, however, and seem to *agree with the prospect* instead. The specific language of transition phrases will help you to do this while still being able to continue your sales call to its conclusion. What we will be doing, in essence, is saying, "You're right, But . . .," which will temporarily soothe the person's ego and help us to retain control.

Canon #51:   *We should be prepared to fully answer all objections, when appropriate.*

There are six major objections that most of us may anticipate having thrown at us during any particular call. We need to be prepared for these interruptions, as well as any others that might occur. They should be considered routine occurrences and should be handled accordingly.

Canon #52:   *We should have answers to objections before us at all times.*

We will see at the end of this chapter how a board system will enable us to access answers to objections immediately in order to keep us fluent on the phone at all times.

Canon #53:   *We should be thinking that there is an answer to nearly every possible objection.*

Surely there may be some objections that are better left unanswered, such as, "Our company is going broke." It would obviously be wiser to wish the speaker in this case good luck in the future and proceed to the next call. Ordinarily, though, we will be called upon to field answers to objections that are new to us. By confidently greeting new challenges armed with the faith that each objection *can be answered and overcome,* we will be more likely to succeed in a difficult situation. Additionally, we will want to study the *format* involved in answering objections that is outlined in Chapter Five, so we can be prepared to fashion our own according to successful principles when the situation requires an original response.

Canon #54:   *When an objection comes during or after our first close, we should answer it, and close again.*

Salespeople sometimes erroneously think that if they *answer* an objection they will be awarded the sale as a matter of course. This isn't so. The prospect still needs to be closed again, and it is the salesperson's responsibility to affix a new close to the end of the answer to the objection in a seamless manner, so there is a continuing flow from the client's interruption to the answer and, finally, to the new close. This is how it works:

Client: [At the close . . .] "Well, I'm really not interested in that."
Seller: "Well, I appreciate that, but did you know that as much as 60 percent of the average business telephone bill is inflated by waste and unskilled communication practices? By investing in these *Telephone Effectiveness Library Cassettes* you'll receive an immediate return that will be visible in your reduced telephone bills.

[Now, closing . . .] But, honestly, I can't describe these tapes adequately, and that's why we invite you to listen to them first, and judge for yourself, okay?"

Canon #55:   *Avoid answering objections that haven't been made.*

Sometimes we feel we are really rolling when answering an objection that has been raised, so instead of proceeding directly to a close, we answer another objection which hasn't been raised. This is not only a wasteful practice, but it is dangerous, as well. The prospect may not have fostered the other objection, but once we have raised it, he or she might start thinking in that direction. For instance, we might say, "And you know, that transmission problem that you probably heard the 1982 models had, well they've corrected it on the 83s." What if the client knew nothing about faulty transmissions? This statement can only make him think, "Gee whiz, have they produced lemons in the past that I should learn more about before making a commitment?"

Canon #56:   *We should know what our goal is for each and every call.*

This may seem to be obvious, but you might be surprised at the number of salespeople who waste their time as well as that of clients by making very open-ended service calls that have a sloppy beginning and that never seem to end. If we are going to make a service call, we should always try to derive *specific* information that will help us to sell something in the future or be prepared to speak about a new service on the same call.

Targets that we are shooting for should be expressed numerically. So, if we are hoping for high sales, we will make specific objectives for ourselves and measure our achievement against these numbers.

Canon #57:   *Make visual reminders to yourself of your goals.*

I like to put signs up at my work station that tell me how many sales or commitments I am shooting for that shift. This really motivates me and aids my concentration. If I work with others, the peer pressure of having them see my target can also be stimulating.

Canon #58:   *Tell yourself, "With each call I am getting closer and closer to my target."*

This self-stimulation is very effective because it keeps us dialing, and it builds valuable momentum.

Canon #59:   *Record the outcome of each call you make or take.*

There is nothing quite as refreshing as having clear data about one's performance during a particular period, as well as when comparing performances across different periods. I suggest we keep a running tally of the number of calls made, busy signals, call-backs, rejections, sales, and objections received. On a separate sheet, we can do an analysis of the resistance we receive by discerning when the objections are occurring in our presentations. Once we can see the pattern of resistance before us, we may then change our presentations to be more effective in the future. Examples of the worksheets to be used for analysis appear at the end of this chapter.

Canon #60:   *Do not resist change.*

As telemarketers, we need to be flexible and adapt to countless numbers of prospects with whom we speak, as well as to constantly changing market influences. By understanding that our long-term security and success depends upon our ability to change ourselves and our presentations in constructive ways, we will not be threatened by novel circumstances and new challenges. Accordingly, telemarketing should be viewed as an ongoing learning experience that can be very stimulating as well as financially rewarding.

The following pages will contain a graphic summary of the telephone sales canons, the Telemarketing Board System™, a general activity worksheet, and an objections analysis worksheet.

After reviewing these pages you'll see how the Goodman System actually works to create a solid presentation through the anatomy of a sales call in Chapter Four.

TELEPHONE SALES CANNONS:

Know	Have	Think	Do	Not Do
Who your prospects are before start of day	All call lists & other tools for organized calling	"Like a pro, I need to prepare my tools to be successful"	Presorting all telephone prospects the night prior to calling	Pluck your prospects out of thin air
95% of what to say before you pick up the telephone	A typed, thorough presentation	"Each talk must sound fresh and spontaneous"	Following the presentation word-for-word	Deviate from the planned talk in the interest of variety
The law of large numbers pays off for telephone salespeople	20 lead cards for each intended hour of calling	"Each call, good or bad, is worth money to me"	Move through call cards in an orderly fashion	Skip around the call cards believing this makes one lucky
Your feelings about selling by telephone are created by you	Visual items around you which inspire you to do your best	"On every call I am getting better and better"	Taking responsibility for your own attitude	Psych yourself out with false beliefs

As many product features as possible	Flip cards or a no-hands written guide of product features	"What are the most relevant features for the prospect?"	Limit the number of features in the talk	Rely upon memory or instinct to mention the features
As many product benefits as possible	Flip cards or a no-hands written guide of product benefits	"What are the most relevant benefits for the prospect?"	Limit the number of benefits in the talk	Rely upon memory or instinct to mention the benefits
Several ways to strategically open a sales call	A list of effective opening lines	"Which opener would work best for this type of prospect?"	Using a planned opener on each call	Wing-it, with a spontaneous opener
Several ways to strategically close a sales call	A list of closing lines	"Which closer would work best for this type of prospect?"	Using a planned closer on each call	Wait for the prospect to close him or herself
A solid method for confirming the strength of a sale when on the phone	A confirmation segment of the talk which qualifies the sale	"I need to test the strength of each sale"	Providing the prospect the chance to express uncertainty	Rush to say goodbye upon hearing the prospect say yes

TELEPHONE SALES CANONS:

Know	Have	Think	Do	Not Do
Methods to diplomatically delay objections	A list of expected objections & answers to them	"I will answer no objection before it is the right time"	Delay most objections if they are made before your first close	Answer any objection before it is time, or argue any minor points
Methods to properly answer objections	A list of effective transition phrases	"There is an answer to every objection"	Answer those post-close objections and close again	Answer any objection without attaching a close-line to it
Your goal for each call & proximity to overall daily targets	Visual reminders of your goals & targets	"With each call, I am getting closer to my target"	Record the outcome of each call; where resistance was aroused, etc.	Fail to learn from calling, and calculate needed changes in approach

Objections Expected With Answers	Telephone Script [Contains the Anatomy of a Sales Call—Four Steps]	Transition Phrases
Price . . .	OPENER	Understand . . .
Competition . . .		Appreciate . . .
Too Soon . . .		Agree . . .
No Interest . . .	DESCRIPTION	Know . . .
Can't Use		Be Surprised . . .
That Much . . .		Agree . . .
Don't Need		
It . . .	CLOSE	*Additional Product Benefits*
Closes		
Assumptive-Choice Check-back	CONFIRMATION	Save $$$$
		Make $$$$
		No Hassles
		Take Charge

Explanation: The TELEMARKETING BOARD SYSTEM ^TM is a no-hands guide to what sales reps should say during 95 percent of their conversations with prospects. By having all pertinent information in front of us, we eliminate unwanted lapses in the flow of our message and may respond to most contingencies as they occur. This system is ideal for installing upright on desks, using plywood or corkboard as building materials.

GENERAL ACTIVITY SHEET

Name:
Date:
Shift:

NUMBER OF CALLS MADE:
COMPLETED PRESENTATIONS:
REJECTIONS:
CALL-BACKS:
BUSIES & NO-ANSWERS:
COMMENTS:

OBJECTIONS ANALYSIS

Name:
Date:
Shift:

NUMBER OF CONTACTS MADE:
OBJECTIONS RECEIVED DURING THE *OPENER*:
OBJECTIONS RECEIVED DURING THE *DESCRIPTION*:
OBJECTIONS RECEIVED DURING THE *CLOSE*:
OBJECTIONS RECEIVED DURING THE *CONFIRMATION:*
TOTAL NUMBER OF OBJECTIONS RECEIVED:

chapter four

The anatomy of a telemarketing call

As discussed in the last chapter, preparation is essential to generating top-flight telephone sales performance. The best way I know to rise to the top and stay there is through the use of what I term the *anatomy of a sales call*—the four essential components of a successful telephone sale.

No matter what your sales objective is or the personality of the prospect, this sequence for selling works, as I am confident you will wholeheartedly agree when you put it into everyday practice. Before describing the formula, though, we need to review a basic assumption about customer motivation.

Prospects desire to be led through a motivated sequence of appeals to arrive at a comfort level where they reward us with the affirmative decision we wish. If we, as salespeople, blow it by issuing a haphazard or nonsensical stream of appeals, we will lose the order or fail to realize our goal for the call.

Don't be deceived, though. Because this is a straightforward method does not mean it is kid's stuff. On the contrary, in its simplicity it requires discipline and attention to nuance and detail. It is more challenging to use than total spontaneity on each call. I believe you will agree that it is better to build a winning formula that increases selling averages than rely upon our wits on every call. As you know, we simply cannot be a genius with every prospect. Our *approach* can be brilliant, however.

In any case, join me as we explore the numbers of ways we may introduce ourselves and product and bring the conversation to a successful close.

THE FIRST STEP: BREAKING THE ICE WITH A GOOD OPENER

It is by now a matter of folklore that traveling salespeople used to maintain the interest of their prospects by swiftly inserting a foot in the door before the portal could be slammed shut. As telemarketers, we are in a more challenging situation relative to winning the attention and receptivity of the prospect.

The telephonic medium is controlled by both parties, either of whom may terminate a call instantly, without notice. If we displease our customers, it is a simple matter for them to cast us into electronic oblivion by depressing a single button. We cannot continue a conversation with an extremely reluctant or agitated prospect, as our traveling counterpart might have done. Consequently, we have the responsibility of developing approaches that artfully engage the attention of the client, while positioning ourselves and our product credibly before the person.

THIRTEEN OPENERS THAT WORK

I recommend thirteen ways of opening a tele-sale. These openers may be blended together in various combinations to give you literally hundreds of unique approaches, as we will discover in the following pages.

As we move along, you will probably notice the extensive use of certain phrases. This is not the result of habit alone. Some of these phrases may appear, at first, to be meaningless chatter. I will explain the reasoning behind the use of these utterances before the chapter draws to a close.

Opener #1:   *The thank-you approach*

> Hello, Mr. Jones? This is Gary Goodman with Goodman Communications in Glendale, California. How are you doing today? Good! The reason I'm calling is to *thank you* for attending our recent Telephone Marketing and Management Seminar at Indiana State University. We hope you found it helpful . . .
>
> Great. A number of folks who attend the seminars leave with a good amount of information, they feel, but they are interested at the same time in keeping up with developments in telemarketing and related subjects. This is why we have developed the new *Telephone Effectiveness Newsletter,* or *TEN,* as we call it. . . .

This method of opening a call sets a friendly tone right away because we are thanking a customer for a decision he or she has already made. In doing so, we are not threatening the prospect with our present request until making the person feel positive about our last service. As a result, the person is placed within a favorable psychological arousal state, from which it is pleasant to consent to further inducements.

We should also note a few ingredients of this first example because they illustrate aspects of all openers.

(A) I address the answering party with his or her name. The name is uttered as a question, not as a statement. It is asked as a question for a few reasons. First, I need to confirm that I am indeed speaking with the correct party. Quite often, a daughter will sound like a mother, or we will wrongly assume an associate who is covering the phones for a person will be the party him- or herself. The use of a questioning inflection in voice also tends to make the call more enthusiastic and spirited in a subtle way. Most folks answer a call somewhat suspiciously unless they have had many positive prior dealings with the caller. Consequently, their tone of voice is rather downcast as the call begins. We encourage vocal doldrums when we utter the name of another without verve or enthusiasm. They respond in a manner that usually matches our tone of voice. If ours is downcast, theirs will tend to be too. If we, on the other hand, sound chipper and eager to speak with the person, she will respond in kind. The use of a questioning tone, because it is directed upward in pitch, is processed as optimism and eagerness to communicate. It is perceived by the listener as a compliment. We seem to *want* to speak with the person.

(B) I always try to ask the other party how he or she is, at the time. This is important for a few reasons. It creates a two-way conversation right off the bat. This is crucial to your success as a professional telemarketer. The number one mark of amateurism in telephone selling is the person who does not involve the prospect in the sales talk at various points in the conversation. I have a residential telephone line that I use exclusively for calling out. I seldom receive calls on the line from people I know. The great majority of calls come from telephone solicitors who are very poorly trained. They begin their sales rap without first being assured they have my attention and interest. As a result, they never earn the order. By asking the other party how she is, we are involving her in the call immediately, independent of her response at that point. Another reason to use this device is that it makes the salesperson sound more self-assured, because he has taken a minor risk of hearing rejection in the beginning of the call. It is true that by opening up the conversation to the imput of the prospect we are increasing the possibility of a negative response from the other person. We will discuss ways to handle such resistance professionally when we discuss methods for handling resistance and rejection in our next chapter.

(C) I try to build client reinforcement into the conversation at every opportunity. Whenever the prospect says something positive about himself or the service I am offering, I will reinforce the statement by saying "good" or "great." This serves as a subtle psychological reward for the prospect and it increases my percentages of being successful on the call.

(D) Believe it or not, grammar takes a back seat to persuasion when we are selling by telephone. I will sometimes build my patterned sales talks on a foundation of disjointed, nongrammatical phrases, if I believe the prospects I am addressing are more comfortable with such bloopers than with the King's English. The theory behind this idea is reminiscent of the old Winston cigarette ads that stirred such a tempest in academic circles some years back. As you may recall, the advertiser claimed "Winston tastes good, like a cigarette should." English teachers across the land were sent into a collective frenzy because, to have conformed to the rules of grammar, the advertiser should have asserted, "Winston tastes good *as* a cigarette should." The word "like" was more effective in selling product, it was believed, because people "talk *like* that." If, however, you are trying to sell something to a snooty prospect, you should strive to elevate your diction, without overdoing it or bringing attention to what you are doing. There is an old adage: Any technique that brings attention to itself is diminished in its impact.

(E) In the thank-you approach illustrated above, I have attempted to move fluidly from my opener to the second part of the anatomy of a sales call, the *description*. This is done by use of a general benefit statement that discusses how telephone seminar alumni wish they could keep up with developments in this interest area. I then proceed to announce the inception of the *Telephone Effectiveness Newsletter* as an answer to this need. My next strategy will be to mention certain features of the newsletter and benefits derived from these features. It is essential that we move smoothly from one portion of the sales talk to the next, creating the feeling that each statement is fueled by the one immediately preceeding it.

As we examine the remaining twelve openers, you will no doubt become increasingly aware of the dimensions that lend our patterned sales talks a sense of directness and motivated order.

Opener #2:   *The after-mailing approach*

I personally like this approach more than many others for opening a cold call or for the purpose of persuading a current client to consider something new.

> Hello, Ms. Jones? This is Gary Goodman with Goodman Communications in Glendale, California. How are you doing today? That's good.
>
> The reason I'm calling is because recently we sent out some letters and brochures, and I was wondering, do you recall seeing one of them?

I love a mystery, and clients and prospects seem to, also. This opener could also be called the "mystery approach," I suppose, because it seeks to engage the prospect in a search for the "missing mailer." Upon being asked about the letter and brochure, most prospects may be heard thinking out loud, "Let's see. Did I get a mailer from Goodman, what? Oh, Goodman Communications." Some folks will flatly say that they did not get it. Others will claim they did, even if one was not sent! In any event, there are a few responses from the salesperson that should be used to propel the call along its proper path. Let's imagine a few responses that the prospect might shoot back at us, as well as our reactions:

Prospect: "No, I don't believe I did get that."
G.G.: "Well, you probably get a lot of that sort of thing in the mail, if you're like me!"
Prospect: "I sure do!"
G.G.: "I know how it is, I just 'round-file' most of it, if you know what I mean!"
Prospect: "I do too!"
G.G.: (Making the transition to the *description*) "Well, it would have told you about a new publication called the *Telephone Effectiveness Newsletter* that promises to help folks like yourself stay in touch with significant developments in the field of telemarketing and telephone effectiveness, which is becoming more important all the time. . . ."

Why did I engage in so much side-talk here about junk mail? The reason I do this is to create *identification* with the prospect— a feeling that I am like her in certain ways. I am also avoiding the typical adversary relationship that exists at the beginning of a call between a prospect and a salesperson. By claiming to treat third-class mail dismally, as she does, I am putting myself on her side. It is no longer a matter of "she against me," but "we against this evil sea of mailers." It works. It also tends to make the prospect laugh a little, which reduces sales resistance.

What would have happened if she said, "Yeah, I think I received that!" We would say:

Great! Our advertising department will be happy to hear that. As you recall, it told you about the new publication called the *Telephone Effectiveness Newsletter,* which promises to help folks like yourself to stay in touch with significant developments in the field of telemarketing and telephone effectiveness, which is becoming more important all the time. . . .

You have probably noticed that I continued in almost the same fashion as when the prospect said she did not get the mailer. It shouldn't matter what is said. We still need to move the other person through the anatomy of a sales call sequence that is so successful in creating sales. Accordingly, it is important to not mislead ourselves. If the person insists she is intimately familiar with the mailer, we will still refresh her memory, because we need to remind her of the benefits mentioned in the letter or brochure that have, by now, been forgotten.

The after-mailing approach is successful because it establishes our credibility while setting up a psychological commitment between the prospect and salesperson early in the conversation. We are credible because seeing is believing in our culture, and we have supposedly established our identity in writing. This persuades the client that we are more real than some disembodied voice that is trying to sell us something on the phone. "Heck," the prospect figures, "if he has gone to all the trouble of mailing something to my attention, he must be for real!" This reasoning, of course, is filled with errors, but this is not important to us. We are interested in being taken seriously, right away, and the after-mailing approach promotes our credibility to help in this regard.

People also tend to feel *guilty* when they throw out a mailing that they have not read. Little did they know that they were going to be tested on it later! To assuage their feeling of guilt, they tend to pay greater attention to our telephone message than they otherwise would have. This means they are working *with* us, during the call, rather than against us.

Opener #3:   *The before-mailing approach*

Although my friends in the printing business will probably throw darts at this book for my saying so, I believe millions of dollars per year are wasted upon the mailers to which we referred above at some length. Why do I say this?

One of the most common cop-outs we hear on the phone is the request, "Well, why don't you send me some literature on that." Sure.

What happens from that point? Does the person requesting the literature really read it and take it seriously? Not often enough, I find. And those mailers that are so easily requested and sent *cost money*, and lots of it, when we add up the total bill from literally hundreds or thousands of such innocent requests.

In seminars I am fond of issuing the following proclamation to participants: "We are not in the *brochure* business!" People seem to mistake the request for a brochure as a sure-fire signal of interest, when it is often a put-off or excuse. So what do I do, refuse requests for brochures? Sometimes. On most occasions, however, I will make the prospect *earn* the piece by convincing me that he or she will really pay attention to it when it comes. Before I agree to send the brochure, I will qualify the level of interest fostered by the party.

Prospect: "Well, you can send me some of your literature on that, if you like."

G.G.: "I'll be happy to, but first let me ask you this: If you really like what you see, how soon will we be able to move ahead with this project?"

Prospect: "Well, actually I didn't say that we would move ahead with any project."

G.G.: "I appreciate that, but are you saying that your firm is highly *unlikely* to embark on a program to improve sales performance?"

Prospect: "Well, right now, and for the next year or so, I think I can say that the answer is yes."

G.G.: "Well, thank you for your courtesy, Goodbye."

I refuse to send a mailer to somebody who will not be a likely user of services, as I have determined this to have been the case from a conversation. Why waste not only money in sending the piece and in composing a cover letter, but also in the fruitless follow-up telephoning that inevitably occurs when we con ourselves into thinking we have a prospect who is qualified to buy.

To avoid these problems, you may wish to use the before-mailing approach to get the most for your buck from the mailers you send.

"Hello, this is Dr. Goodman calling. Who is the person there who handles sales training? Is that the General Sales Manager, or someone else?

"Fine. And what is her name, please? Good. Is she in? Thank you.

"Hello, Ms. Embry? This is Dr. Gary Goodman with Goodman Communications in Glendale. How are you? Good. The reason I'm calling is because I am going to address a letter to you and I wanted to make sure it will be routed properly.

"By the way, you are the person who authorizes all sales training there at the plant, is that right? Good. Is there anyone else who has to sign-off on sales training programs there? You're it, huh? Great.

"Before dropping this in the mail, allow me to ask you this . . ."

I will continue in this vein until I am convinced that I have reached the buyer or buyers, and that they "deserve" a mailer. The preliminary questions help me to qualify the need for my product or service, while giving me information in such crucial areas as to whether the firm can afford my services and how soon they might use them. I then set priorities for following up the written materials with a telephone call.

I also have an opportunity when using the before-mailing approach to focus the attention of the prospect upon a certain portion or portions of the mailing. This is helpful in generating commitment from the other person to take my cause seriously.

Opener #4:   *The new service approach*

"Hello, Mr. Smith? This is Gary Goodman with Goodman Communications in Glendale. How are you? Good.

"The reason I'm calling is to tell you about a new service that we have underway here that promises to help you to increase profits. It's our *Telephone Effectiveness Library* which is a series of audiocassette training tapes geared to helping you better service customers, while making new ones by phone. . . ."

This is a very straightforward approach. The hook here is the word "new." Everybody wishes to stay abreast of developments that can enhance the profitability of a business. By telling the person that we have something new we are expanding his horizons, while providing the opportunity to seize a potential market opportunity before the competition does.

Opener #5:   *The bargain approach*

"Hello, Mrs. Probst? This is Gary Goodman with Goodman Communications in Glendale, California. How have you been? Good.

"The reason I'm calling is because I recall you wanted to arrange a training program there at the plant a few months ago, but the cost of travel was prohibitive, am I right? Right. Well, I have some good news. Because I intend to be coming through Cincinnati in a few weeks, I'll be able to make a capsule presentation to your staff for a fraction of what it would otherwise run. Sounds good, doesn't it?"

This approach is sometimes used by companies that find they are over-stocked on a given item. They will call people and tell them they have an oversupply situation, and offer, at a discount, supplies that would otherwise cost more money. Some companies have done so well with their over-stocked presentations that they have made this pretext a staple in their marketing campaign.

You may note that I introduced a new wrinkle into this presenta-tion—a *trial close*. I mentioned the major benefit of consenting to my ap-peal, saving money, and then proceeded to observe, "Sounds good, doesn't it?" If she says it does, I will proceed to select dates for performing the program and carry on the conversation as if it is only natural that we are going ahead with the date. If she offers an excuse or resistance, I will re-sell the benefits of the program and attempt a more traditional closing of the call. We will discuss closing techniques in detail later in this chapter.

Opener #6: *The inactive account approach*

"Hello, Mr. Frisbee? This is Gary Goodman with Goodman Com-munications in Glendale. How have you been lately? Good.

"I was looking over some materials the other day and I noticed that we haven't had the privilege of working with your firm for several months, and we were wondering if there was a reason for this that I should be aware of." (Pause for answer)

We are obviously on a fishing expedition with this opener. We may hook a big one, or we may come up with an old boot, instead. In any case, we will have made an important contact with a paying client who seems to have lost the urge for doing business with us.

As you can imagine, if one client has become disenchanted with us, it stands to reason that there is a situation of which we should become immediately aware if we are going to remain financially viable. Perhaps a competitor has undercut our prices. It's possible that one of our staff angered this important customer and may have unknowingly aroused the wrath of countless others. No matter what the cause of the silence, our call will probably be viewed as a positive gesture that could restore a former client to the active list.

When using this approach, we should be prepared to field anything. For instance, if our client retorts:

> "Yes, there *is* a reason you haven't heard from us. Your products keep breaking down, which is proving to be too much of a headache. We don't need the aggravation!"

We should be prepared to respond with a conciliatory comment that is designed to reassure the person that the problem has already been, or will be remedied. Our rejoinder might be:

> "I respect that, Mr. Frisbee, and I would like you to know that we have already undertaken the task of setting that area straight. I give you my personal assurance that this problem will never happen to you again, and to give you the highest possible guaranty of service, I am going to ask that you place your future orders through *my* office, and I will personally oversee your account, okay?"

You might be surprised how likely it is that a formerly burned client will consent to giving us another chance if we approach the matter delicately. It is very possible that he or she is unhappy with the replacement supplier and is looking for a rationale to rejoin forces with us.

Opener #7:   *The survey or marketing research approach*

> "Hello, Mr. Friendly? This is Gary Goodman with Goodman Communications in Glendale. How are you? Good.
>
> "The reason I'm calling is because we are doing a bit of marketing research and we would appreciate your opinion on a few matters pertaining to the training of salespeople. I only have a few quick questions, that should take two minutes to respond to, okay?"

This is an unusually worded approach, in some ways. Normally, I recommend that we avoid asking permission to continue a conversation with a prospect. For instance, it is unwise to call someone and ask, "Are you busy right now, because if you are, I can call back later." This is *asking* for rejection. Nonetheless, when using the survey or marketing research approach, I recommend we obtain the permission of the other party before proceeding because we are going to ask for rather sensitive information. If the prospect believes we are going to immediately turn around and use that information to sell him, we will be cut off quickly.

The remaining portion of the survey approach opening may be devoted to at least two styles of questioning: (1) We may ask a short series of questions that immediately whets the appetite for our product or service; or (2) We may ask more subtle questions for the purpose of gathering intelligence to be used in preparing a subsequent call or mailing effort. If we elect to arouse interest and satisfy it on the first call, we need to do so in a fashion that is not too obtrusive or strident, given the dignified opening strategy we employed. For example, the conversation might continue in this way:

"First of all, do your salespeople receive any on-the-job training in the area of telephone selling? I see.

"Do you believe telephone selling is a cost effective means of generating leads and new business? Okay.

"If you were to obtain information on telephone selling, would it be through audiocassettes, videotapes, or live seminar training? Very good.

"Your responses are very interesting, because what we do is this . . ."

All I really need to do, now that I have zeroed-in on his attitudes, is to propose that I have what he wants, in the desired medium, be it audiotapes, videotapes, or live training. My most likely approach would be to further qualify the prospect to determine if he has a training budget and to find out how to best deliver the product to his organization. I might settle for an appointment or go for the gusto and try to reach agreement by telephone, which will be confirmed by a letter known as a "written memorial" of our transaction.

Some companies are reluctant to divulge information to people performing telephone surveys. I employed a male graduate student to telephone selected industries and ask questions and gather data similar to the items contained in the present example. He started by calling the paper industry in Los Angeles and found he was getting nowhere fast. I replaced him with a female who claimed she was doing research associated with a university, which was true, and she obtained all the data I required. I tend to believe that the men who were answering the phone felt threatened by a male's voice, in this instance, where they were not nearly as agitated by a female voice. Moreover, in the first case, the prospects were apparently afraid that the survey had been commissioned by a competing company, and they were not going to cooperate in placing themselves in jeopardy.

The survey approach is helpful because it allows the prospect to sell him or herself through the process of answering questions in a given way. Some communication theorists argue that all persuasion really takes place as an outcome of people *convincing themselves,* rather than being convinced by someone else.

Opener #8:   *The emergency or urgency approach*

Some sales professionals maintain that people make buying decisions only when they think it is imperative to do so. If, in other words, they think that they have "all the time in the world" to make up their minds, that is precisely how much time they will require before acting.

The role of the salesperson, then, is to "set a fire beneath the prospect," by convincing her that she must act now to either get the product at all, or receive it at a reduced price. To make this appeal plausible, salespeople sometimes resort to rather bizarre strategies. One of them employs the "misshipment pitch," favored by some office supply companies.

> "Hello, who is the boss there? Henry? Is he in? Yeah, I'll hold. Tell him it's long distance calling. Thanks.
> "Hello, Henry? You're the boss there, aren't you? Good. Henry, I have a little problem on my hands and I know you can help me out. I just sent out a small box of Bic ballpoint pens to an account of mine there in Cleveland. You are near 38th Street, aren't you? Good. Well, my accountant called me this morning, after I sent the pens out, and told me my client has just declared bankruptcy. What do you think of that? I know. In any case, I've already paid the freight on the pens one-way, and if I have to bring 'em back, I'll get stung both ways. You know what I mean? Good. Well, I was thinking you folks use Bics, don't you? Great. Listen. If you will take the pens I'll give them to you at my cost, and I'll pick up the freight, Okay?"

This isn't a bad pitch—if there had been a bankruptcy to begin with. The trouble is, there was no such event, but scores of telephone rooms across the country trick people into acting based upon similar tales. If this is such a deceptive practice, why do I include it on my list of openers?

It's important to not only develop appropriate sales strategies, but also to be warned against others that can put us at a disadvantage.

We should examine this appeal dispassionately to discover what makes it successful. First of all, there is tremendous *enthusiasm* emitted by the salesperson. This is electrifying. It induces the cooperation of people who would otherwise be unmoved if appealed to cooly and rationally. Moreover, it is aimed at the boss, or the decisionmaker. The salesperson knows she can write up the order based upon the consent of the person on the line, and this increases motivation. Perhaps most importantly, it appeals to the bargain-relishing nature of most prospects who will grab at opportunities to save money. The suggestion that opportunity only knocks once is implicit in the emergency or urgency approach. "Act now," the salesperson is saying, "or forever regret this missed opportunity." When these persuasive elements are put together, and presented convincingly, they can be irresistible to many otherwise sober and conservative prospects.

Some sales professionals insist that without a sense of urgency, it is all too easy for prospects to offer the common excuse, "There's no hurry. I'll think it over." The urgency approach denies the validity of this excuse.

Opener #9:   *The referral approach*

"There is no greater salesman than a satisfied customer," we are told by conventional wisdom. This is very true, if the satisfied customer tells other people of his or her good fortune. Many happy folks will give us the name of a friend or business associate to follow up and call. If we are smart, we will use the strength of the referral as much as we can.

> "Hello, Ms. Jasper? This is Gary Goodman with Goodman Communications in Glendale, California. How are you? That's good.
> "A mutual friend of ours, Ian Barrington, suggested I give you a call, because he thought I may be able to help your organization as I have helped his. What we do is this . . ."

You may have noted that in this example I have attempted to place the persuasion on Mr. Barrington's lips and not on my own. I said, *"he* thought I may be able to help your organization as I have helped his." It is very difficult for the prospect to argue with the utterance of an esteemed, and not present, friend. Consequently, she is likely to accept the promise that I can be of assistance without contest.

There is something very important about the referral method that should be discussed. It is easy for me to place glowing praise upon myself if I put the words in the mouth of a disinterested third party, as I have begun to do above. I cannot as easily praise myself, though, without sounding pompous. For example, I can easily get away with the claim that, "Our customers praise the quality of the programs that we produce and indicate that our products are light-years ahead of anyone else's." If I took it upon myself to compare my services with a competitor's directly, without the third-party testimonials, I would seem to be putting down the other supplier, which breaches business etiquette.

Opener #10:   *The demonstration approach*

"Hello, Mr. Montana? This is Gary Goodman with Goodman Communications in Glendale. How are you? Good.

"The reason I'm calling is because we are the people who publish the very popular and useful audiocassette series, the *Telephone Effectiveness Library.* For a limited time, we are making these very useful tapes available to organizations on a trial basis.

"The tapes are really handy because they show you how to increase profits in all areas of the company, from customer service to inside sales to outside sales. Specifically . . ."

A demonstration approach relies on the merit in the adage, "the proof is in the pudding." By encouraging the temporary or partial use of a product, with satisfaction guaranteed, we encourage people to purchase from us over the phone, while reducing the number of steps required from our first customer contact to the final delivery of the product.

What would happen if we tried to obtain a one-call close without a no-risk demonstration offer? We would meet with more resistance, and would generate substantially fewer sales. Telephone selling is like mail-order selling in the past. Sears made a name and reputation for itself, while establishing the direct-mail marketing industry in this country, by giving a money-back guarantee to its catalog customers. This assured millions of Americans that the firm they "couldn't see" was, in fact, reputable.

I recommend the trial or demonstration approach whenever you are attempting to penetrate a new market with a novel product. The most convincing thing you can do is to put the product in the person's hand. A telephone call, followed by a swift delivery by mail or messenger of the product, will reap benefits.

I suggest you place a definite time limit on the free use of the product. Depending upon the product, you may select a period such as seven, ten, or fifteen days from receipt. The implication you wish to convey is that if your product is unsatisfactory for any reason, you will be notified within the time allowed for examination.

If you get the feeling that the prospect will simply take advantage of the temporary use of the product and return it without serious consideration, it is obviously wasteful to send it out in the first place. I suggest you employ a bottom-line qualifying question if you are in doubt about his seriousness by the end of the call.

> "Just so we're clear then . . . If you find the product is everything I have said, you will send me a check, right? Great. Thank you very much. . . ."

I grant that this question may sound a little harsh, perhaps, but it is designed to produce *clarity* and *commitment*. Through its use I tell the prospect that I am in business to generate revenues, and not merely to engage in futile postal exercises and incur needless expenses. Do not be afraid to ask this kind of bottom-line qualifying question. It will save you a lot of hassles, and will be taken gracefully by serious businesspeople.

Opener #11:   *The premium approach*

Have you ever noticed the most magical word in print advertising is the word "free"? It's true. Look at the most appealing ads and you will probably find this term or its equivalent. Whether we admit it or not, we all love free gifts, even if they are only those tiny toothpaste tubes that Procter & Gamble test-markets by mail.

When we offer somebody a free gift over the phone, the same type of good feeling is generated.

"Hello, Ms. Baxter? This is Gary Goodman with Goodman Communications in Glendale. How are you? Good.

"The reason I'm calling is because we are sending folks such as yourself a free cassette training tape, which covers the subject of telephone etiquette and customer relations, as a way of introducing our seminars to a larger audience. Sounds good, doesn't it? Well, great. . . ."

I might proceed to inform Ms. Baxter about our more extensive cassette libraries, newsletter, or seminar services, depending on my objective and her apparent receptivity to the free tape offer. I could also use the tape as an example of the quality of information we impart, and request a personal interview, at which time I will present the tape to her.

I am familiar with insurance agents who offer free health-condition identity cards to potential major-medical policy purchasers. I have even heard of the technique whereby certified life underwriters, who are encouraging investments, send a crisp dollar bill to an executive with a note that reads, "This is the first of many dollars we hope you will make with us. Sincerely . . ." They then follow up the mailed premium with a phone call. I have been told that nobody forgets the gesture. Some do ask for seconds, though.

Opener #12: *The special occasion approach*

"Hello, Mr. Decker? This is Gary Goodman with Goodman Communications in Glendale, California. How are you doing this morning? That's good.

"The reason I'm calling is because we're celebrating our two hundred and fiftieth week in the business, and we thought you would like to be a part of the festivities. (You see, in the consulting business, we measure our tenure in *weeks,* not years!) What we have in store is this . . ."

You may have observed that it is unusual to announce such a minor event to a prospect or client such as an anniversary, but I would assert that this can provide a very light touch to the beginning of a call and serve to loosen the resistance of the other party rather quickly. Public relations people are masterful at inventing what an author once called "pseudo-events," or events that do not occur naturally but are fashioned by those of us who wish to create them. We should feel free to invent these "happy pretexts" for calling prospects, as they sound festive and spontaneous, which gets people in the mood to buy.

Opener #13:   *The new idea approach*

This approach may be one of the most straightforward around. There are a few variants of this format:

> "Hello, Ms. Elliott? This is Gary Goodman with Goodman Communications in Glendale. How are you? Good.
>
> "The reason I'm calling is because I conduct seminars in the area of telemarketing and customer relations, and I thought it would be a good idea to get in touch with you to see what we may do to pursue the prospect of bringing in-house training to the Elliott Company."

This appeal may seem a little simplistic to seasoned salespeople, at first glance, but I assure you that in its directness, it is often very successful. It rather clearly sets forth who I am and the service I provide, while making the general assertion that I "thought it would be a good idea to get in touch . . ." I have never heard a negative response to this opener, such as, "Well, I think it is a terrible idea to get in touch with me." People tend to believe somebody who asserts an empty phrase such as this.

You may have noticed the phrasing I used toward the end of the opener. I indicated that I was calling to see what we may do to "pursue the prospect of bringing in-house training to the Elliott Company." This is soft-selling language. To "pursue the prospect" sounds like I am inviting an aristocrat to polite conversation over a cup of tea. This language is not used by accident. If I were to use stronger language with prospects who are strongly committed to a code of civility and decorum, as are, say, college deans, my message would not be received nearly as well as when I choose more delicate wording.

Although it is very subtle, I am actually closing the sale with this phrase, because I am assuming agreement on the concept of programming, while waiting for information regarding *how* that programming may best take place. Invariably, the prospect responds with the statement:

"Well, I will need to see some written materials and get a better idea of how the programs are financed, and so on."

When I hear this response, I know I am more than halfway home. I promise the materials, discuss financial arrangements, and proceed to set dates, *assuming* the materials that will arrive by mail will be in good order.

We will discuss the desirability of being assumptive when we cover the subject of closing later in this chapter.

The second variant of the new idea approach makes reference to a recent event or new application of a product or service to a client's situation:

"Hello, Mr. Lewis? This is Gary Goodman with Goodman Communications in Glendale. How are you? Good.

The reason I'm calling is because I ran across an article in one of the newsletters I subscribe to that I thought you would be interested in, and which gave me an idea for helping your organization to be even more profitable."

This sort of "thinking-of-you" introduction can be very effective. People like to believe that others are thinking positively and constructively about them. Are you at least momentarily enchanted whenever somebody you like tells you he or she had a dream about you? This opener appeals to the ego in a similar fashion.

Mix' em and Match 'em As You Please

Now that you have these thirteen openers, you are limited only by your creativity and imagination in implementing them. Have fun by mixing and matching them. For example, the after mailing and new service approaches are natural companions, as are the inactive account and new idea methods. I'm sure you will find that by having solid openers, the remainder of the sales call tends to proceed smoothly.

THE SECOND STEP:
THE DESCRIPTION PHASE

The opener will capture the attention of the prospect, however it is just as important to focus the thinking of the buyer on the product or service itself. Unlike face-to-face selling we don't have all the time in the world to physically demonstrate a product or tout its attributes. We need to compress what we say into an attractive package and move on to ask for the commitment we wish.

There are some basic suggestions for formulating the descriptive phase of the sales call.

Sell Benefits and Not Features Alone

People seldom purchase products and services based upon what these items *are*, but rather based upon what they will *do for them*. Salespeople, on the other hand, tend to believe that it is the other way around, that if we run off at the mouth about infinite numbers of product features, the prospect is bound to make some meaning of this for herself. Not true. Let's look at the example of an automobile.

Many car salesmen boast about the fact that a car is turbocharged. In and of itself, turbocharging is meaningless. What will it *do* for the buyer? It will give the buyer: (1) plenty of passing power on otherwise hazardous hills and highways; (2) peace of mind, knowing that he or she may respond quickly to road hazards and challenges; (3) more fun from driving, because the car feels like a sports car; (4) social status, because the Turbo is the top-of-the-line model and other drivers know it; and other benefits which the salesperson may announce.

We should all brainstorm a list of benefits that our businesses provide to clients. I know that you think your company has probably already done this, or has come up with an exhaustive list, but think again. You would be amazed at the number of firms that don't have any idea of what the consumer is *really* buying from them, relative to benefits, at a given time. Sometimes, what were benefits in the past cease to be advantages in the present and future.

Once we have a list of benefits, *we should choose two to four benefits to discuss within a telephone sales presentation. No more.* The reason we should limit the number is because we need to save time on the phone, and because people buy based upon the salience or importance of benefits to their immediate situation, not based upon the number of benefits presented.

What if your product or service has no benefits, to speak of? This is nearly impossible, but if you are selling a commodity that is well known and available almost everywhere, you will need to be more creative in building your list. You will also want to focus the attention of the buyer upon *secondary gains* of doing business with you, such as prompt service, delivery, and general responsiveness; special billing of the account; certainty of supply; and so forth.

I often recommend to clients the following exercise. Write out on a piece of paper all of the goals that an individual or company may have at a given time. Having written out these things, proceed to build a case for why your product or service satisfies each and every need in some fashion, no matter how much you believe you are stretching the facts. I am sure you will discover latent and significant benefits to clients that you never thought of before. These benefits may then be selectively introduced into your telephone sales calls to test their merit. Build on the ones that work, and discard the rest.

Make Your Description Conversational

One of the most common errors made in writing telephone sales presentations, generally, and descriptive phases, specifically, is that they sound stilted and artifical to the listener. They sound this way because they have been written out and not spoken out.

Spoken language differs substantially from written language. When we undertake to write something, we become more formal, and our language reflects tension and discomfort. When we speak, on the other hand, we are more casual and often more direct. These qualities put prospects at ease, while our literary habits cause uptightness and may impeach our credibility, if it sounds like we are reading from a script.

To sound spontaneous, I suggest you compose your descriptive phase of the script with the assistance of a tape recorder. *Talk* your presentation into the recorder and play it back to yourself. If any language sounds too stiff or formal, substitute more appropriate terms until your patterned appeal flows naturally.

Keep It Simple, Salesperson (The Kiss Method)

Many of us are fond of telling stories about how we or somebody else talked himself or herself out of a sale. It happens all too often. *We* know so much about our wonderful products and services that we simply must tell everything we know over the phone. If we do not resist this temptation, we can lose a lot of sales.

To avoid this, I suggest you keep your presentation *short*. In most cases, the shorter, the better. Linguists tell us that 50 percent of the En-

glish language is redundant or repetitious. (Sometimes redundancy rein-
forces a point, as it is designed to do in the preceeding sentence.) For the
most part, redundancy on the telephone is irritating and costly. People
expect conciseness through this medium and are impatient when we repeat ourselves unnecessarily.

The following exercise will help you to eliminate redundancy.
Write your sales presentation. Afterwards, go back and draw a pencil
through every other word in the presentation. Try to read what is left.
It will be a little rough, but you will probably derive 80-90 percent of the
meaning contained in the longer draft. Restore a few of the essential
words, and you will be left with the bare bones of what you need for an
efficient patterned talk.

How long should your entire talk be? It should not normally exceed
three minutes, and if your purpose is to set an appointment rather than
sell a product on the call, the length of the conversation may be as short as
two minutes.

Use Motivating Language

If we sound bored with our product or service, we may rest assured
that our buyers will be also. I am always impressed with how enthusiasm
is really contagious, as is its opposite. We need to choose enthusiastic
terms to describe our wares. For instance, if we are saying to a prospect
that she will realize "a savings from using our product," this statement will
probably get a ho-hum response. If we claim that the savings derived from
our product will be "significant," or "substantial," or "meaningful," we
are on our way to generating a positive response from the prospect.

There is an old injunction that is offered to salespeople: sell the
sizzle. This means that if we are in the restaurant business and we want
to sell steaks, we need to capture ways of describing the aroma, flavor, and
other sensory benefits of our fare. Without these terms, people have every
good reason to settle for hamburger.

THE THIRD STEP: CLOSING THE SALE

The closing of a sales presentation is often called the most important part
of the venture. We see newspaper want-ads for closers who have the ability
to cement commitment to a proposal quickly and effectively. What is

meant by closing, and what are the most effective ways to do it on the telephone?

The close is that part of the presentation where we ask for the sale. The method we use in asking, however, is crucial in determining our success.

There are three basic closes I recommend: (1) The choice close; (2) the assumptive close; and (3) the assumptive-checkback close. By relying upon these three closing styles, you should be prepared to handle any telephonic sales situation.

The Choice Close

This close is usually the first that is learned by new salespeople. It is helpful because it compels a prospect to think in terms of *how* he wants a product, rather than *whether* he wants it. Automotive salespeople are frequent users of this technique when they ask us if we like "the blue car; or will the red one be better?" By limiting the available choices to two alternatives, the seller is eliminating the possibility that we don't want a car at all.

The choice close works very well when setting appointments on the telephone, as this illustration will demonstrate.

"What we do is this, Ms. Bolton. We reserve a few minutes to stop by your office and show you the details of the training program, so you may have a first-hand perspective on the benefits of telemarketing training.

"The calendar suggests a good time to come by will be tomorrow afternoon between two and three, or will Thursday morning be better for you?"

The nature of the choice allowed in this example is clear. She may elect one of two possible appointment slots. This is a very advantageous way of scheduling because we avoid throwing our entire calendar open to the prospect, which makes us appear to be unpopular and unsuccessful, plus it helps us to maintain a sense of control over the conversation and selling situation.

You may have noted some rather interesting closing language that I inserted with the words, "The calendar suggests . . . ." Note that I have avoiding saying, "I would like to stop by and speak with you," or "a good time for me will be," as such phrases emphasize the salesperson and cause an unnecessary confrontation between our mutually possessive calendars. Instead, we give the calendar a life and voice of its own. The *calendar* is doing the appointment setting here, not human beings! The calendar, consequently, may be much more assertive than I may appear to be, and it will get away with it. When was the last time *you* argued with a calendar, anyway?

There is a drawback to relying exclusively upon the choice close. First of all, not every product or service suggests a neat division into choices which are acceptable to a prospect and salesperson at the same time. This reminds me of the time when a bandit snuck up on the stingy Jack Benny and demanded; "Your money or your life!" Benny reportedly answered, "Let me think about that for a minute . . ."

The second drawback to using the choice close is that it is so well known and popular. If your prospect perceives that you are closing her, she may react negatively to your transparent strategy. For this reason, I suggest you equip yourself with a few alternative closes that are as effective, and sometimes work even better.

The Assumptive Close

My consulting work takes me around the country. While this can be exhausting sometimes, there are other times when rare opportunities present themselves. I was heading back to California from the East and had a short, two-hour layover at National Airport in Washington, D.C. Having been to that exciting city a few times before, I discovered a wonderful restaurant in nearby Alexandria, Virginia. I always longed to be able to fly into a city like Washington or San Francisco merely for the purpose of having a wonderful meal, and then go on my merry way. Well, it seemed that providence was going to make this possible, and that I would indeed be able to feast on veal marsala and fettucini in the nation's capitol.

I called a hotel limo which picked me up at the airport and deposited me right in front of the restaurant. Things were going perfectly, and I was going to have about an hour to enjoy my meal. I walked in the door, and noticed that a table by the front window was available. *That* was the place to sit, because you can see the strollers outside on the cobblestone streets. I approached the maitre d', and, sensing that he was going to hustle me off to an interior table in the darkness beyond, I said; "Dr. Goodman, table for one." I immediately began to walk toward the table I wanted next to the window, and started to sit down before my guide could fully articulate his objection. As I moved like a panther toward its prey, I could hear him mumble something about reservations and another party, but he reluctantly pulled out my chair to assist me by the time we reached the window. I proceeded to have my dinner in peace and splendor, caught the return shuttle, and continued my journey with pleased palate and happy heart.

What is the moral of this story? I knew that the host would not give me the seat I wanted if I acted in any way as if it was undeserved. By acting *assumptively*, my will, at that moment, superceded his own. The same principle supports the power of the assumptive close.

> "What we'll do is this Ms. Bolton. We'll reserve a few minutes to stop by your office and show you the details of the training program, so you may have a first-hand perspective on the benefits of telemarketing training.
>
> "The calendar indicates a good time to come by will be tomorrow afternoon between two and three. When we sit down to discuss the program, it will be handy for me to look at your most recent phone bills to determine how we may save you some money. That won't be any problem, will it? Good."

I have modified very little from our example of the choice close to illustrate the meaningful differences between the two approaches. The assumptive close places the burden of decision making upon the seller and not the buyer. It is the seller who asserts what time the meeting will be, as if such a declaration is only natural. Moreover, the salesperson should continue speaking about a minor prospect's behalf. In this illustration, I have gone on to ask if the prospect will dig up a recent telephone bill, which is an easy mission to accomplish, and which will not, in itself, be objectionable. By agreeing to produce the phone bill, the prospect has implicitly agreed to the appointment and to the stated time.

I have also modified some language in the passage to make the entire closing segment more positive. For instance, I have changed the words. "We reserve," to the more powerful and active phrase, "We'll reserve." This gives the section a greater sense of momentum and makes the client feel that a decision has already been made and preparations are underway. It is more difficult to stop a moving object than to prevent an object from moving at all. The calendar, accordingly, went from *suggesting* in the choice close illustration, to *indicating* in the latter closing effort. Again, the language is stronger.

There is an important idea operating behind the use of assumptiveness. People hate to make decisions, and when they are put into the position of making an affirmative or negative decision on a matter that requires change, they will usually opt for the status quo and reject the new approach. It is the smart salesperson who avoids the sticky area of choice by making the decision for the prospect in the least obtrusive way.

Some folks find the assumptive close too aggressive. For those who do I believe I have the best of both worlds in a close that is both powerful in its assumptiveness, while allowing the buyer a degree of choice in the matter. This close is called the *assumptive-checkback* close.

The Assumptive-Checkback Close

"What we'll do is this, Ms. Bolton. We'll reserve a few minutes to stop by your office and show you the details of the training program, so you may have a first-hand perspective on the benefits of telemarketing training.

"The calendar indicates a good time to come by will be tomorrow afternoon between two and three, *okay*?"

The wording is almost exactly as it was in the assumptive close, except here we make the decision for the prospect and add the word, "okay". Why use the word "okay"? We are conditioned to say "okay" when we hear someone ask, "okay?" To be effective in the closing context, we should use it as if it is an afterthought that we are checking with the person. If you prefer a phrase to substitute for "okay," try, "fair enough?"

A phrase I like very much is; "Sounds good, doesn't it?" Prospects find it nearly irresistible. I remember giving some on-the-spot coaching to an inside sales rep who was trying to write up a sale with a hard-to-close buyer. I was whispering in her ear on the sidelines, but this was to no avail. Quickly, I seized a scrap of paper and wrote, "Sounds good, doesn't it?" and told her to say it right away. Without hesitating, she blurted it into the receiver. The other party said, "Yes, it does," and the sale was hers. Remember this closing phrase if you ever find yourself in a situation where you need to engineer assent quickly. I think you'll find it very handy.

Now that we have examined the three parts of the sales call that produce compliance, we should examine the *confirmation*, which assures it.

THE FOURTH STEP:
CONFIRMING THE SALE

Inexperienced telemarketers share another performance characteristic: they rush off the telephone instantly upon hearing the prospect say yes. This is problematic, because we need to reinforce the positive decision by following six steps.

Congratulate the Buyer for a Wise Decision
We noted in a prior section that buyers find decision making a noxious state. This is true. Moreover, the time immediately after someone has made a buying decision is very sensitive and meaningful, because buyers often begin to suffer from pangs of remorse for the decision they have made. As a result, if their misgivings are not alleviated by the salesperson, they will unravel the agreement. To avoid this, the salesperson should immediately say something like, "good," or "great," or "fine" after the prospect has said yes to the offer. This will give him instant gratification rather than punishment for his choice in the situation.

Clarify Delivery or Fulfillment Details

"Just so we're clear, then, we'll ship your cassettes to 8353 Third Street, Suite 305, Los Angeles, 90048, is that right? Good."

Although this seems unnecessary if you are staring at their letterhead or business card, you might be surprised how often businesses move or request an item be sent to a branch location. Checking delivery details also confirms in the client's mind that you do have an agreement at this point.

Repeat the Terms of the Offer to Create Clarity
Listening research indicates that as much as 50-75 percent of what people hear is *never processed consciously*. This means that we may have

been perfectly clear on a telephone call by our own standards, yet have confused the listener or have been dealing with a "space cadet" who was tuned into a different planet when we were speaking. Therefore, it is crucial that we repeat the basic aspects of our offer.

> "As I indicated, the cassettes will be coming to you on a guaranteed basis. If you are dissatisfied with them for any reason within seven days of receipt, simply return them. Of course, when you find them to be satisfactory, we will appreciate being paid by return check as soon as possible."

Provide the Buyer With an Opportunity to Ask Questions

Some salespeople believe that it is better to disallow questions because we might otherwise provide an opportunity for the buyer to withdraw from the sale. I believe it is important to provide just such an opportunity. If we railroad the order, the client will probably not pay us when it is time to do so, and we may lose our product, as well as invest many dollars in collection expenses. It is far better to handle a hostile or negative question before we have added a client to the books than later. We can also resell the person on the benefits of the product or service, thus creating satisfaction where it is needed.

Sense the Strength of Commitment to the Sale

Some prospects will say yes to us simply to get us off of the phone. We need to develop a "telephone ear" to become sensitive to people who are not serious. If you have any doubts about the strength of an order, I suggest you ask a final qualifying question to resolve the matter.

> "Fine, Ms. Appleton. If you like our product upon receiving it, you won't be reluctant to send us a check for it right away, will you? Great."

In fundraising situations, donors often commit to a larger pledge in the heat of the moment than they are able to fulfill. We might approach such a person this way:

> "We appreciate your gift, Ms. Appleton, yet we would like to make sure that it won't be a burden for you . . ."

By waiting for a reply, we will probably receive a proper clue as to the appropriateness of the gift. If it is too much, we may always settle for half or a portion of the original amount.

Restore Goodwill by Leaving the Buyer with a Positive Feeling About the Transaction

We noted before that selling can be an adversary, me-against-you situation. After we have vanquished our commercial foe or purchaser, we need to make the call end on a light note, if possible. This does not mean that we should blurt out some bawdy stories, but that we should make friends again with the prospect. It is as if we are trying to return to the sense of rapport that was created in the opening phase of the call. To accomplish this, I suggest we use the following line:

> "Fine, Ms. Appleton. I'd like to thank you for your time *and your patience;* I appreciate it; and I hope you have a very good day, okay?"

I have emphasized the words, "and your patience" for an important reason. By this time, the buyer is getting a little impatient, so in recognizing this fact, we are giving her a compliment as well as being polite and thoughtful. You will be surprised at the number of folks who literally giggle when you use this line. It is as if we are reducing steam from a pressure cooker. The buyer will probably thank you in return, which is always a good sign of a strong sale. I have added a final "okay" simply to sell the person on having a good day, as well as to provide me an opportunity to hear any possible discontented tones of which I should be aware.

When we have moved the prospect through this series of four steps in the anatomy of a sales call, we have orchestrated a proper telephone sale.

PUTTING IT ALL TOGETHER

Now that we have analyzed the essential ingredients of a sales call, what does the entire format look like?

Here is a patterned sales talk that incorporates the suggestions and phrasing mentioned above. Can you pick out the opener or openers that have been used? How many benefits appear here? What sort of close is used? Perhaps you would elect to use a different one. That's fine! Did I sufficiently confirm the sale? You be the judge . . .

"Hello, Mr./Ms./Mrs. Reader? This is Gary Goodman with Goodman Communications in Glendale, California. How are you today? Really? I'm sorry to hear that. I hope you feel better.

"The reason I'm calling is because recently we sent out a letter and brochure and I was wondering, do you recall seeing that by any chance? You don't. Well, that's not too surprising. I mean you must get a lot of that kind of thing in the mail, am I right? Right.

"Well, it would have told you all about our new seminar, called Telephone Marketing & Management, which is being offered through a number of universities across the country. What it does is show you and your staff how to open new accounts and get more business from the ones you have, as well as save time and money in the process. Folks tell us it's the best program they have ever attended because it's practical and down to earth.

"What we're doing is this. We've scheduled a public seminar in Chicago on June 7, and we have reserved three seats for participants from your firm, and we were wondering whether three will be enough, or if five would be better?

"Fine, then we'll keep it at three, and just so I'm clear we'll send this confirmation to Tracy Reader, Abba Zabba Manufacturing, 310 Wacker Drive, Chicago, 60611. Great. Along with the confirmatiom will be an invoice for $275 per participant for a total of $825. Do you have any questions I might answer? Fine. I'd like to thank you for your time *and for your patience*, and wish you a wonderful day, okay? Goodbye."

Simple, right? It really is, when you get used to its structure. You may have been asking yourself, what about handling incoming calls? Can this format be used when others call us? It sure can.

HOW TO HANDLE INCOMING CALLS EFFECTIVELY

There is an unfortunate distinction that most organizations maintain between incoming and outgoing telephone calls. While it is true that some communication dynamics are altered when someone takes the initiative to call us, rather than the other way around, *we would do better if we behave as if we called the party*. Why is this so?

There is usually excessive passivity among those who are asked to handle incoming calls. Very often, they are not regarded as salespeople at all, but as clerks, order processors, and, sometimes, customer service employees. These terms are misleading because these people are put in a terribly responsible position. Sometimes they are held responsible for account maintenance or development but are not given the sales skills with which to do a good job. Consequently, they treat an incoming call as a passive exercise where the caller is the one who is given control of the conversation. It should be otherwise.

What is *different* about an incoming call? When the other person calls, we may infer he or she has some prior knowledge of or interest in the product. Moreover, this party has a specific question to be addressed or agenda that he or she wants us to cover. Fine, so far.

We get into trouble by not taking control of the conversation ourselves. All we need to do is allow the caller the opportunity to provide us with the *opener*. We should then be prepared to pick up the ball and move to the next three phases: *description, close,* and *confirmation.* This is how it might sound if someone called me asking for information about my Telephone Marketing and Management seminar:

Caller: "Hello, I read about your new telephone selling program, and I was wondering when it will be offered next in Chicago. We have a few people who may wish to attend."

G.G.: "As you may know, this program is offered through a number of universities across the country. What it does is show you and your staff how to open new accounts and get more business from the ones you have, as well as save time and money in the process. Folks tell us it's the best program they have ever attended, because it's practical and down to earth."

"What we're doing is this. We've scheduled a public seminar in Chigago on June 7, and we'll be happy to reserve three seats for participants from your firm, or, I was just wondering, will five be better?"

Note what happened here. I elected to resell her on the benefits of the product before announcing the date and closing the sale. Most recipients of this call would merely announce the date of the Chicago program, without announcing benefits or attempting any close. In neglecting to properly execute a descriptive, closing, and confirming sequence, a significant selling opportunity is lost or postponed.

Although my example does not show a confirmation, I would have moved through the same procedure that I employed in structuring the completed outgoing call presentation.

YOU SURE MAKE IT LOOK EASY

In exploring the anatomy of a sales call I have presented a "best case" illustration. Life doesn't always proceed so smoothly, you have probably observed. You're right!

We need to be prepared to handle flak from our prospects in the form of objections and excuses. We will explore ways that you may effectively handle negativity and resistance from clients in the next chapter.

chapter five

How to handle resistance and objections

The previous chapter outlined a "best case" scenario for selling by telephone in which we assumed that the prospect was a willing party to the sales transaction. As we know, customers are quite a bit tougher and more resistant to persuasion than we gave them credit for. This chapter should fill out our analysis and show several methods for handling resistance and objections as they occur.

Before disclosing my most favored method, I feel it is only fair to outline for you some of the many theories that have been advanced by different selling philosophies in terms of how to manage interruptions during the sales message.

THE ADVERSARIAL THEORY

The adversarial school of thought positions the salesperson as the antagonist of the prospect. This is a manipulative point of view in the sense that we, as salespeople, are doing everything we can to beat the client in the verbal battle that is the typical sales encounter.

For those salespeople who subscribe to this school, the telephone call is thought of as a battle of wits, or even a shouting match, in which each party is more concerned in proving he or she is right, than in effecting the closing of the transaction. People who are adversaries believe that a sales *really* begins after the prospect has uttered some dissatisfaction.

As you have no doubt guessed, the adversarial method tends to sound abrasive and contributes to the bad press telephone marketing receives among businesspeople and consumers.

THE NONAVERSIVE THEORY

This notion suggests that people are sick and tired of being *sold* everything, from gadgets on TV to airline bargains on billboards. Consequently, people are going to blow us out of the water if we sound like we are trying to sell them anything. The best way, then, to overcome their substantial resistance is to anticipate it and defuse it within the context of our sales appeal. In other words, we should identify the ground of probable resistance and eliminate it rhetorically before it has a chance to fester and defeat our sales strategy.

This is how such a defusing procedure might sound:

Salesperson: Hello, Mrs. Jones, this is Gary Goodman with Goodman Carpet Cleaning in Glendale. How are you? Good. The reason we're calling is to let you know we are coming out to folks' homes to clean one room free of charge! Now that you've heard that, you're probably thinking, okay, if it's free, what's it going to cost me, right? Right. Well there's nothing to be concerned about because . . .

What the salesperson is doing is trying to think like the customer and speak the customer's language. This creates identification and trust and can open the door to a sale where one had been previously shut. This is also called a *two-sided message strategy* in which we are trying to raise an opposing point of view on the one hand and proceed to shoot it down on the other. This can work well if we think the client fostered some negative impressions about ourselves or our industry before we called her or she called us. For instance, some of the people in the home improvement industry have been maligned because some less professional colleagues would say almost anything to get a sale. Well, if we are trying to sell aluminum siding to someone who heard about a neighbor getting burned by someone in the same trade, we will be wise to use a two-sided message to create a distinction in the mind of the prospect between ourselves and the less legitimate predecessor. We might say something such as:

Salesperson: Hello Mrs. Jones? This is Gary Goodman with Perpetual Aluminum Siding here in Glendale. How are you? Good. By the way, you folks are probably used to getting calls from people in the siding business, am I right? Well then, I bet you've heard some pretty interesting sales appeals, right? (After listening for the tales of woe . . .) Well, I know how it is . . . You see, the reason we're calling is because we have something our customers have been thanking us for bringing to their attention. What it is is this . . .

As you can see, the nonaversive approach involves the customer in the beginning of the call to help us to overcome her resistance. We want her to breathe a sigh of relief because we're not one of the bad people.

We do need to be careful, though, when we use the nonaversive approach. If the prospect did not foster a negative predisposition to communicate with us before the call, we might inadvertantly cause one to be developed during the call. We should consider doing some initial market research to determine if the reception we are likely to get will be negative, neutral, or positive, and if it isn't negative, we should use a one-sided strategy only and save the nonaversive method for another time.

THE CONSTRUCTIVE THEORY

This idea indicates that the customer is really our friend, and when he or she resists, what is really happening is *interest* is being shown in our product. Handled properly, such a sign of interest may be turned into a closed order. Rather than becoming flustered, as might be the response of many salespeople, we should happily answer the objection, expecting that our answer will sufficiently pave the way for a sale to result.

I find this notion problematic because it tends to encourage us to answer *too many* objections from prospects who are really lifeless and have no chance of turning into orders. There are simply some people who are so firm in their resolve *not* to buy that they cannot be persuaded otherwise, and we need to manage our time effectively by recognizing this and moving on to the next candidate.

THE CLOSING THEORY

Closely aligned with the constructive theory noted above is the closing theory that says that when an objection is raised, a closing opportunity is presented at the same time. What the prospect is seen as saying is, "Look, if you can overcome this problem I have, you will win the sale."

This idea is acceptable if the objection is uttered at the end of our appeal. What happens, however, when we have just called someone, and five seconds later the person claims that he isn't interested? We will be in trouble if we attempt to answer the objection at that point, because we really don't know what the person is or isn't interested in. If we try to handle the objection then, we will seem to be fighting or arguing with the buyer, which doesn't succeed very often.

THE ESCAPIST THEORY

I have actually heard this one advocated by a self-styled telemarketing "expert" in a seminar. According to this theory, whenever we hear someone object, irrespective of the nature of the claim, we should rush off the phone without delay and call the next person on our list. The idea is that there are enough fish in the sea, and given the law of large numbers we will happen upon someone who has virtually been waiting for our call in order to purchase our product or service.

This approach is fraught with mistaken assumptions. One is that there are unlimited prospects to call and that we will never exhaust our lists. As you know, there are situations in which we might only have dozens or a few hundred candidates to call, and we cannot let them go so easily when they object. Another assumption that is advanced through the escapist school is that if you are really presenting a good pitch, you shouldn't have to encounter many objections because there just won't be that many. To me, this is like training firemen and telling them, "Look, if you're really good firefighters you won't have to learn how to use a water hose because you'll avoid fires altogether."

THE "ALL IS NOT WHAT IT APPEARS TO BE" THEORY

This is also known as "the objection *behind* the objection" school of thought that says that people do not really tell salespeople what their *true* objections are at first. Instead, they tend to throw at us a phony excuse that is really a smokescreen. Savvy salespeople, consequently, aren't tricked, and ask the prospect, "Is there *anything else* that might be keeping us from going ahead with this plan?" Sometimes prospects will then reveal that their companies are broke, or that they are dealing with another supplier because he is the brother-in-law of the owner, and you don't stand much of a chance to get the business as a result. This approach is useful if you feel that you are hearing a hollow excuse instead of a true objection.

THE "HEAD IN THE SAND" THEORY

This approach suggests that we simply *ignore* the objections we hear, as if they never occurred, and continue our sales talks as if nothing happened. In other words, if we pay no attention, it will go away.

I have an aunt who swears by this approach in social encounters. If she hears a question from someone and she feels that she doesn't want to venture a reply, she'll act as if she didn't hear it to begin with. She finds that folks aren't bold enough, in many instances, to try again, and they drop the matter, instead.

As you can imagine, this procedure could alienate a good percentage of the people with whom we speak. In fact, I think that this is an approach typical of the unprofessional telephone solicitors who give the sales medium a bad name. Acknowledging interruptions is essential to decency and effective communication with clients.

THE "I'LL TALK 'EM TO DEATH" APPROACH

This is also known as the "shotgun" or "machine-gun" method because through it a salesperson sprays a nonstop barrage of benefits and features at the client in the hope that the person won't have enough of an opportunity to interrupt. Also akin to the "I'll wear 'em down" school, the talk 'em to death procedure gives the prospect but one out: to buy, or forever have *no* peace.

THE NEGOTIATION THEORY

Here we assume that "everybody has a price" and that the salesman will be able to close the order if he can only determine what the client wants to pay. To learn the necessary information, the salesman will ask, "What did you have in mind, in terms of what you thought would be appropriate to pay?" which allows the client to "sell herself."

A variant of the negotiation method is to simply throw up one's hands and ask the client, "What would it take for you to buy this service?" which will encourage the person to reveal vital information that enables the seller to close the order.

THE "MAKE 'EM REPEAT IT" METHOD

The idea behind this approach is that customers aren't thoroughly convinced of the merits of their own objections, so if they are asked by the seller to repeat their interruptions, they might crumble instead, or weaken in their resolve. This serves the added purpose of clarifying what the real objection is. In doing so, salespeople avoid the tendency of answering the *wrong* objection, which can irritate the customer and cause orders to be lost.

If a salesperson is using the "repeat it" method, all he or she has to do upon hearing the objection is ask, "What?" or "I'm sorry, would you repeat that?" I have even heard some salespeople ask "Why?" which forces the client to justify her objection. Rather than face the discomfort involved in explanation, the prospect may balk instead, and give in to the persuasion of the salesperson.

There is a chance that in repeating the objection the client may be *reinforcing it* instead of weakening it. With particularly strong-willed folks, this may occur more frequently than otherwise.

THE BANDWAGON APPROACH

This is also a very powerful method of selling benefits in which we tell the client:

A. "I understand how you *feel;*
B. "A number of others have *felt* that; however,
C. "They *found* that it really wasn't so. In fact, they were pleased that we offered such a reliable service, which is another good reason to approve this plan, okay?"

Also referred to as the *"feel, felt, found"* strategy, this procedure essentially tells the prospect that he is right in objecting, as others certainly have, but he will be pleasantly surprised to find what they have discovered. What we are saying to the resister is that he is in good company and there is nothing to fear.

Whenever we can use third-party testimonials in our presuasion we are usually better off for the effort. People want to feel that they belong to a larger group of like-minded folks and that they won't be the first to take the plunge into what might be regarded as a risky venture.

THE GOODMAN METHOD

My method assumes certain things:

1. Most objections are uttered too soon by prospects, who really are *anticipating* that they won't like what they are about to hear in the presentation.
2. Most salespeople *answer* objections too soon, and get so sidetracked from their presentations that they are unable to smoothly return to where they left off.
3. If a prospect can be persuaded to listen to a sufficient amount of the pitch, he will have enough information upon which to make a yes or no decision.

4. No objection should be *truly answered* until we are prepared to use the answer as a part of a close.

There are two very simple rules in using this approach: (1) If an objection is uttered *before* you have reached the first close, delay it with the use of a transition phrase and return to the text where you were before you were interrupted, and (2) If the objection comes *as you reach the close* or *as you are closing*, use a transition phrase, give a good answer to the objection, and close again.

I am going to provide an example of this method in action. Paragraph #1 will outline a short presentation without interruptions, so you can sense how it should proceed. Paragraph #2 will introduce objections that will appear in brackets, and you will then be able to see how to *delay answering* the objection before the close, how to answer at the close and proceed to close again.

Paragraph #1:   *Script with no objections*

"Hello, Mr. Jones? This is Gary Goodman with Goodman Communications, in Glendale. How are you? Good.

"The reason I'm calling is because we have come up with something that will help your staff to stay on top of vital information in the field of telemarketing. It's called the *Telephone Effectiveness Newsletter,* and what it does is this. . ."

Paragraph #2:   *Script with objections and responses*

"Hello, Mr. Jones? This is Gary Goodman with Goodman Communications in Glendale. How are you? [I'm not interested.] Well, I'd be surprised if you were at this point, but the reason I'm calling is because we've come up with something that will help you and your staff to stay on top of vital information in the field of telemarketing. It's called the *Telephone Effectiveness Newsletter* (I don't have any time to read.) Well, I appreciate that, but what it does is this . . ."

You probably noted how smoothly we can revert from the buyer's objection back to the presentation by using a simple phrase or two known as *transition phrases.* All of the transition phrases I use follow the same format, which starts with the word "Well" and continues to *agree with the prospect*. This is crucial, because we don't want to appear as adversaries and turn off the listener or have the phone slammed down in our ear. By *agreeing* with the client we are defusing the objection and taking a "side by side" orientation with her, rather than "squaring off" with her.

Here are some very useful transition phrases that I encourage you to use:

1. Well, I understand that, but . . .
2. Well, I appreciate that, but . . .
3. Well, I know what you mean, but . . .
4. Well, I respect that, but . . .
5. Well, I agree with that, but . . .
6. Well, I'd be surprised if you were at this point, but . . .

Once you know the format, you can invent transition phrases on your own. Try to avoid using the same transition phrase twice during the same call, as this can sound like a ploy and diminish its impact.

Looking back at the examples given in Paragraph #1 and Paragraph #2, we should note that I only *delayed* the objections because I hadn't reached my first close. Here is how I would have answered the objection, "I don't have any time to read," if it had occurred at the close instead of before it.

G.G.: "What we're doing is sending out a trial copy of the *Newsletter* and we're so confident you'll want to continue, that we will schedule you for receiving the remainder of the year's editions at our reduced cost unless we hear from you to the contrary, which is your privilege. But what we say is enjoy the free copy, and see what you think, okay?"

Client: "I don't have any time to read."

G.G.: "Well, I understand that, because we're all so busy these days trying to stay ahead of soaring costs and diminished revenues. That's precisely why the *Newsletter* is so helpful, because within its tight pages each month you'll learn how large and small companies are cutting costs and making record profits through savvy telephone use. But, honestly, I can't describe it adequately on the phone, so enjoy your first copy, and then decide, okay?"

What if the person raises another objection at this point? Clearly, I have an option to answer it or to gracefully let the person off the hook by going on to the next call. I allow my "telephone ear" to tell me whether there is still some life in the prospect or if I will be better advised to move on. I take it, in other words, on a case by case basis.

When working with one rather prestigious corporation, we found that *fully 80 percent of our gross sales came after we delayed or answered one or more objections.* As you can see, it behooves us to press on if we think that there is a chance that a sale may result. In no case, however, will I continue if the person sounds adamant or if I have already answered three objections. There are limits to anyone's patience that should not be overstepped.

THE SIX MAJOR OBJECTIONS
THAT YOU WILL HAVE TO ANSWER

Objections usually come in familiar forms. Specifically, you should expect to encounter these:

1. Your price is too high.
2. I am dealing with your competitor.
3. It's too soon to buy.
4. I'm not interested.
5. I can't use that much.
6. We don't need that at all.

How can we effectively deal with these, once we are prepared to answer them? One of the best methods for treating objections is to *change the base of thinking of the prospect.* Here's how it works. Imagine that your client has just said, "Your price is too high." There are several options as to how to respond. First of all, you can change the customer's base of thinking or frame of reference by stating that this service shouldn't be viewed as an expense, "but as an investment that will yield definite results." Here we are altering the buyer's focus on expenditures and substituting an expectation of revenues. We can also deal with this objection by using what has been called the "pennies a day" approach, where we break down the grand total that something will cost into smaller units of measurement. We can ask for clarity by inquiring why the product or service seems to be too expensive. We might even consider using one of the truisms that abound in the language of commerce, such as, "Well, you know you *do* get what you pay for," and "It's true, quality does cost a little more." Along this line, one may assert that what one pays for something initially and its ultimate cost may be different things entirely. For instance, we have all had the experience of buying a cheap product that breaks down or doesn't do the job, only to find that we have to replace it prematurely. This may have had a lower price initially, but its operating cost was greater than the higher priced alternative. Finally, we can deal with the price objection by being "snooty," and by insisting that "It's true that our service isn't for everybody, only for those who recognize and appreciate its value." Sometimes, price is "its own reward," and we buy designer jeans or scents or even chocolates because there is a snob appeal attached to being able to splurge on such an item.

One objection that we all have to deal with, unless we have a "monopoly" on a product or service, is when someone claims that she is considering or actually using one of *our competitors* to supply her needs. What can we do? One temptation to avoid is "knocking the competition." We should avoid this because it insults the customer for having made a bad decision. Feeling criticized, the same person is unlikely to embrace our offer.

I am comfortable with the idea that our competitors are "okay, but we're a little better." This sets us up to be generous in our references to competitors, yet still distinguish our unique benefits to the customer. It is sometimes helpful to ask the client, "What is it about them that you find especially helpful?" and then sit back and listen to the response. We can learn things we never thought of before, while listening for unique openings or opportunities that we can take advantage of before our competitors do. Once we have determined why the client is doing business elsewhere, we may proceed to offer the same item at a more favorable price, or probe to discover and subsequently satisfy needs that aren't being met by our adversaries.

When asking what someone likes in the competition, be prepared to hear some unexpected replies such as, "Well, we really like those free trips that we can earn from them by purchasing so much of their product during a given period. Last year, we went to Hawaii!"

Some of us hear that *"it's too soon to buy"* because what we are peddling is purchased by the account only during certain budgetary periods. If this is the case, our persuasion should occur well in advance of those periods so that we get the business when it is finally awarded. By staying in touch with clients we are not only setting up a sense of commitment to us, we can also use their guidance to tell us how and what we should try to sell when we have the chance.

Others hear it's too soon to buy because the client is really saying "Look, there's no urgency, here. We'll be here tomorrow, and so will you." What we are being told is that we *need to create a sense of urgency* by suggesting to the client that the offer may not last until tomorrow, or that the price may be increased, or that the commodity may be bought by someone else. Unless there is some degree of scarcity suggested by our presentation, the client may luxuriate in complacency and end up never buying from us.

When we hear the line, "I'm really not interested," we are hearing someone tell us that he hasn't heard enough benefits to be persuaded that the product or service is going to do him any good, or that we chose the wrong benefits to tout. In either case, we should delay the objection if it comes before the close, in the hope that upon hearing more information the party will naturally become interested in what we have to sell. If the objection comes at or after the close, we should ask a probing question or two to determine where we went wrong. I like to ask, "If it could be shown to you that you will make more money by getting into telemarketing, is this something you'll probably want to learn more about?" If the person then says no, I realize that he is not being reasonable, and can't really be sold. If yes is the answer, I will then go on to show how the need to make money can be addressed through my service.

Often, clients will tell us, "Hey, you're loading me up; I can't use that much." One of the best ways to deal with this objection is to simply say, "Fine, I'll only send you half," if you are selling a commodity that can be broken into smaller units. If you really believe that it is in the client's interest to purchase the whole lot, you can establish a usage pattern with the person right there on the phone by asking, "How much do you have on hand right now?" After getting the figure, and recalling when they last ordered, you can forcast how long the proposed new supply will last. By breaking down the order into mathematical units in this manner, you will find a lot more buyers going along with your recommendations on purchasing certain quantities.

When I hear, "We don't need that at all," as I reach the end of the presentation, I recognize that I have missed the mark and have not really communicated with the prospect. Either they have not understood me and the proposed benefits of my offer, or I have misunderstood them and their needs. What I do in this case is stop myself, as I did in the "I'm not interested" illustration, and ask, "Now just so I'm clear, you folks *are* interested in saving on your telephone expenses and making your salespeople more productive, am I right?" After hearing the usual affirmative reply, I will say that this is precisely what my product or service will help them to accomplish. Sometimes we need to remember that clients may not be responding to the merits of what we are offering, but instead may be tuning us out entirely. Therefore, when they claim they don't need something, they may really be saying, "Look, I didn't listen to you, but I *probably* don't need whatever it is you are selling, anyway."

HOW TO HANDLE
THE DIFFICULT OR IRATE CLIENT

Sometimes clients fly off the handle over a number of things. They may simply disagree with our claims, or they may be angry over a past transaction. They could also be confusing us with the last hundred or so people who called them selling everything from bibles to baubles, and I have frequently had suspicious folks ask me, "Didn't you just call me last week?" In any case, conflict is sometimes the result of dealing with buyers. What can we do when they get angry?

There are several tips for defusing the angry client. For a thorough exposition of this area see the Customer Relations chapter in *Winning by Telephone*. First, what we should avoid doing is taking the matter personally, or defensively. It isn't unusual for an angry client to try to levy a few personal criticisms against us, and our normal reaction is to fight back with a few choice words of our own. Instead of giving in to this temptation, we should focus our attention on problem solving. Let's imagine the customer says, "Goodman, you're a bozo. In fact, you are so *bozaic* that one might say you're filled with *bozemetry*. In my clinical opinion, you are a prime candidate for a *bozectomy!*" Now, I'm sure you'll agree, this sort of exchange could make one feel that he isn't liked. Instead of responding in kind, we should say something to the effect, "Well, I'm sorry to hear you say that, but let's see where we can go from here." In other words, we should keep our sights on the future, rather than harping on the past with mutual allegations of having caused each other harm or hassles.

One particular communication technique known as "active listening" can help in this kind of circumstance. What we do when using active listening is try to discover what someone really *means* by *repeating to the other person's satisfaction what we think he or she meant*. In a way, we are trying to repeat what we think we heard them say, without judging the content one way or the other. In the illustration made above, I might have responded by saying, "Well, it sounds like you feel that I acted like a bozo, which caused you some inconvenience. Is that right?" Then, I shut up, and let the other party emote, and let off a little steam. You'll find that the other person not only calms down, but also respects you for allowing him to explain his feelings. Moreover, we usually hear things we never knew about, which can help us to achieve clarity and orient ourselves to the present situation.

Sometimes it really helps to defuse conflict if we simply *admit blame*. By listening to the complaint of the other person and responding with, "Well, it sounds like I just blew it there," we can help the situational mending process considerably. Our customer will think we are a big person for doing so, and our relationship may be stronger for the exercise.

One thing to remember is that conflict is inevitable and we shouldn't blame ourselves for finding that there are frayed emotions between ourselves and clients. The key is how effectively we cope with the situation. By concentrating on the future and constructive alternatives instead of blaming personalities, we can turn a losing proposition into a learning experience and a threshold of new mutual understanding.

The Goodman Method of handling objections gives us rules to govern how to handle resistance in most of the situations we will encounter. I encourage you to write out in script form all of the objections you expect to meet, along with meaningful and fluent responses. You will then never be at a loss for words in the most challenging circumstances when marketing by phone.

chapter six

Managing
telemarketers

If you have been asked to oversee a telemarketing function, and you have any degree of tenure in the job, you already appreciate the unique challenge of running such a program. There are probably several issues that are currently presenting themselves, from where to find the most capable phone reps, to compensation plans that reward achievement. This chapter will address what I have found to be the most critical areas for generating a highly productive telemarketing program.

HOW DO WE GET STARTED?

It is a lot simpler than you think to get started in a telemarketing program, although many telephone companies will try to convince you otherwise. First of all, you don't need any fancy telephone equipment or WATS lines to generate a pilot program, which is what I recommend you initially strive to produce. All you need is a clear idea of your goal and your potential or actual market.

IDENTIFYING YOUR MARKET

You probably have a good idea about the type of people or companies that are going to support your product. What you now need to do is arrange a way of getting intelligence on those people. The sort of information you need is their telephone numbers, addresses, key buyers and executives, and, perhaps, their annual revenues and total number of employees. To determine these facts, the best place to look is in a business, trade, or professional directory.

Most companies are listed in one directory or other. For instance, there are directories dealing with electronics and manufacturing representatives, service industry companies, traffic executives, national trade and professional associations, and others. In fact, there are probably enough directories available to keep your staff busy for centuries.

I suggest you consult two sources to find the directories of interest to your organization. The first source is human: your reference librarian in the largest public library or university library in your community. To give you an idea of what such a person may do for you, imagine this scenario. You have just had the bright idea that the people who are most likely to buy your product are in the videotape business. You first look in the Yellow Pages under videotape, but there are scattered listings of retailers and others of little use to you. What you're after is people who make and distribute videotapes. By a stroke of genius, you ask yourself whether your librarian would know of a source. If you are fortunate enough to be in Los Angeles at the time, you could call the downtown branch of the L.A. Public Library and ask to speak to someone in the business directories section. After waiting on hold for several minutes, you will be given one of the best treats in your professional life—a very competent human being who can (1) tell you if such a directory exists; and (2) invite you down to the library to see it if it is in; or (3) give you the name of the publisher so you may purchase it for yourself. The Los Angeles Public Library, for one, is stocked to the brim with valuable, otherwise elusive directories that can mean gold to you and your telemarketing function.

The second source I recommend is the book by Bernard Klein called *Guide To American Directories*. This is an actual encyclopedia of directories which can show you, in one step, whether your market may be collected in this form.

Directories are handy in many ways, but, as you recall from a former chapter, they are sometimes inconvenient to use. I find them tough to read sometimes, especially when I intend to proceed by calling one number after another. I prefer to use index cards or their equivalent, because they are easily read and follow-up comments may be written on them.

Another commonly used source is the professional list broker. This is the person whose business it is to locate or collate lists that clients need for doing mailings, telephoning, or both. A list broker may be found in the Yellow Pages under "mailing lists," or "business mailing lists."

Sometimes, lists will be available in the form of mailing labels, and you will be required to pay extra to have the data put on 3" x 5" index cards. Many lists offer addresses and company names only. In other words, it may be up to you or your staff to look up the telephone numbers to make the lists serviceable. In many cases, lists will not have the names of the decisionmaker or functionary you require. For instance, you may wish to reach people who could be found in what is casually referred to as a complaint department. Specifically, you want the manager of this department. Well, this may not be information contained in the data base.

List brokers may purchase lists from anyone, and often do so to serve the needs of a particular client. In addition to brokers, there are mailing list houses that have one main list for sale that they own and have collated. For instance, they may have a list that is broken down into S.I.C., or Standard Industrial Classification codes. So, if you want to contact insurance sales offices or lawyers or colleges, the list company or broker would be able to program the computer to give you the names available within the geographical area in those occupational categories. There is one drawback in dealing with a mailing list company instead of a list broker. The former may wish to sell you only his list, and fail to advise you to obtain a preferable list that is not owned by his company.

A purchased list will cost you between $35 and $95 on the average if you have the information printed on mailing labels. If you prefer cards, the price may escalate to a few hundred dollars per thousand cards.

There are, of course, cheaper sources of names, but you may be losing some valuable information in relying upon them. For instance, there are the good old Yellow Pages. Unfortunately, they may not contain all companies in your marketing universe, and they come without the names of executives and mailing zip codes, in most cases.

Telephone companies publish "reverse directories," or street address directories, as they are formally called. What they do is give you the names and telephone numbers of all of the businesses and consumers on given streets in the city directory you have rented. For instance, the first page will be Apple Street, and the street numbers will appear in ascending order until all of the businesses and consumer names have been itemized. These directories are handy in the sense that sales territories may be managed efficiently by zip code classification. If your telemarketing crew is interested in setting appointments for subsequent follow-up visits, it is very convenient to assign pages from the directories to specific representatives.

If you are calling a large territory that is served by more than one telephone company, you will need to make separate arrangements with each company for renting directories appropriate to their service areas.

Once you have obtained your lists, you will want to acquaint yourself with the subject of *territory management.* Telemarketing reps are notorious for claiming that certain areas or types of companies are "no good." Don't believe them. While it may be true that there are depressed areas or industries, it is more *constructive* to maintain that each territory is no better than any other. Failing such an assertion on the part of management, you can face reps who require wasteful pampering and cajoling simply to do their jobs. Be firm on this point!

Sales reps also have a nasty habit of skipping through call cards because they do or do not "like" certain names on the cards. Tough luck. I suggest you require them to systematically move through their call cards, as was mentioned in a previous chapter.

WHERE DO YOU FIND
TOP-NOTCH TELEMARKETING REPS?

A participant in one of my seminars decided to start a telemarketing unit in the company he owned. Without advising me or anyone else, he proceeded to do the logical thing. He ran some classified ads in the *Los Angeles Times* under the designation, "telephone sales." He later reported to me his tale of woe—all he ended up drawing from the ad were what he termed "flakes, deadbeats, and sharpies." I couldn't resist giving him one of my infrequent "I told you so's."

He chose one of the worst areas in the newspaper to advertise for telemarketing reps. There are a few reasons this is so. First, most folks who put ads in the telephone sales column are from "hard-core" companies that are in the ball point pen, photocopy machine supply, or so-called advertising business. There are special organizations that do nothing but high-pressure selling of these items on a nationwide basis, largely through outbound WATS lines. Through use of the emergency or misshipment approaches that we discussed in Chapter Four, they end up pulling the wool over thousands of eyes per week. The salespeople who work in these firms are usually a pretty hardy crew who can withstand the rigors of a straight commission deal requiring factual distortion and cunning creativity. Alumni from these firms are looking for a fast buck, in the main, and are not the proper candidates for representing companies that strive to be more forthright and conventional in their approach.

The existence of the "boiler room" type of operation gives a black eye to other companies that are trying to do a constructive job on the phone in opening new business. A latent effect of the tainted reputation of telephone selling is that many upright job seekers avoid calling ads listed under the "telephone sales" designation in the classifieds. In other words, your best candidates may be avoiding calling you! What can we do about this?

I suggest you run your ads under other categories in the newspaper. For example, if you are hiring part-time or part-time and full-time reps, place an ad under the heading, "part-time." You will attract more conventional personality types through this device. Accordingly, you should insist that your other ads run under the general heading, "sales," and not *telephone* sales. It will appear that you are offering a better job.

You may wish to consider using smaller community newspapers as well as college papers to attract your labor force. I have found college students to be energetic workers, who respect the extra spending money that a telemarketing job can supply.

The very best telemarketing reps, however, seem to be actors, by most accounts. They appreciate the job, because they are out of work so frequently, and they are often excellent communicators who can adjust to different people on the phone, while making a script sound as if it is being uttered for the first time, every time. If they are real pros, they can also take criticism constructively, and respond quickly to suggested changes in strategy and approach.

You can persuade actors to come to you by mentioning that your job is "ideal for college students, actors, part-time moonlighters," etc.

Another approach is to call the actor's union local in your town and ask if you can post a notice advertising the job opportunity. They will, no doubt, welcome your interest.

When actors *do* get work in their main profession, for instance, in television commercials and the like, it is only fair to give them a leave of absence to do their part, and then return. This sort of flexibility can build gratitude and result in a long and mutually rewarding relationship. In one situation with which I was associated, certain actors were on the selling staff for a period of years before changing jobs.

College employment services can be good places to contact for the purpose of finding employees. Some departments can prescreen your candidates before recommending them to you, which saves time and money. I would try to first telephone the people at particular colleges, and in cases where you have not been terribly successful in promoting your cause, you may wish to visit them in person.

HOW LONG SHOULD REPS BE ASKED TO WORK?

I have been associated with all kinds of telemarketing environments. Probably the least successful companies are those that require reps to work a conventional eight-hour shift. What is wrong with the normal workday, you may be asking.

Telephone selling is unlike any other kind of sales job or any conventional occupation. By nature, it is filled with an activity cycle that is extremely demanding. A given rep may speak to twenty or twenty-five people an hour, while making from eight to fourteen completed presentations within that time. That's a *lot* of communicating! Not only is the rep required to "tune into" different personalities and emerge successfully from vigorous screening, but she is asked to do so beautifully, on each and every call, with very few breathers in between. This can be, very simply, quite grueling. Eight full hours of this effort is literally too much for the average person.

If a company insists on using an eight-hour shift, I guarantee it is not receiving eight hours of value for its investment. People will be pacing themselves, and the pattern of production will be distributed as follows, assuming an average daily output of ten sales:

9am - 10am:	2 sales
10 am - 11 am:	3 sales
11am - Noon:	3 sales
Noon - 1pm:	Lunch
1pm - 2 pm:	1 sale
2pm - 3 pm:	1 sale
3pm - 6pm:	0 sales

It is obvious that the major amount of production is coming in the morning hours, when the rep is fresh and ready to go. Her production will dip toward the lunch hour, and will reach an afternoon high between 2 and 3 P.M. after her lunch has settled, and prospects have returned to the office after theirs. From 3 P.M. on, until closing, the typical rep who works an eight-hour shift will probably be worthless in terms of productivity. This failure to produce may be attributed jointly to physiological exhaustion and sensory overload. In any event, you don't have to put up with it, or pay for it, if you don't want to.

HIRE PART-TIMERS
AND MAKE EVERYBODY HAPPY!

Perhaps the best approach to the performance curve is to respect it by hiring part-time workers who can physically sustain performance over, say, a four-hour period, instead of an entire workday.

This means that you are going to be spending a good amount of time recruiting, because the turnover among part-timers can be heavier, and because you will need more "bodies" to fill your available phoning hours.

You will also find, if you restrict weekly work shifts to four or five hours per day, that you may save a good chunk of money on employment benefits, such as health insurance. This adds up, as you know.

The pool of workers available to you may very well expand if you use part-time shifts. If you call consumers in the evenings, for example, you may find that sales professionals who are interested in moonlighting for extra money will join your team, as will otherwise capable people. Parents of schoolchildren may be able to go to work between the hours of

9 A.M. and 1 or 2 P.M., because their toddlers are in school during those hours. College students and others may populate your 1 to 5 P.M. shift.

One of the most important "hooks" in attracting and retaining quality personnel is your compensation package. You may find it very attractive, as have some extremely successful telephone operations, to offer the opportunity of "full-time pay for part-time work." To make this offer real without jeopardizing your finances, you will want to put together a compensation plan that rewards production.

"BEHAVIOR IS A FUNCTION OF ITS CONSEQUENCES"

There is a fundamental maxim in behavioral psychology that "behavior is a function of its consequences." This means that *behavior that is rewarded will be repeated.* Most of us are familiar with the wisdom of this notion, but we seem to forget it when we construct pay plans for employees, and especially telephone communicators.

Many pay plans are structured on a straight-salary basis, where people are compensated at a certain level of dollars and benefits, irrespective of the degree of positive performance they execute. This means that the person who does a superior job is paid the same amount as the laggard. That is, until the annual review comes, and the achiever is given a measly 10 percent pay raise against the laggard's 8 percent. The company figures that this year-end comeuppance will set the books straight and motivate future performance. This sort of thinking is dead wrong.

First of all, a straight-salary compensation plan rewards poor performance exactly as it rewards good performance—inaccurately. The achiever is underrated, while the laggard is overrated. Both employees are given a reinforcement signal that says, "Here's your pay—keep doing what you're doing." It should come as no surprise that production stays the same, for a while, and then tends to curve downward, because there is also no negative reinforcement to prevent a slump across the board among employees. The threat of firing may be used, but this sort of negative motivation may produce temporary compliant behavior, but it will not motivate people to get up the gumption to perform at higher levels.

Another approach, of course, is the straight-commission pay plan. A friend of mine is a millionaire salesman, who is fond of saying, "Any salesman worth his salt is a straight-commission man. He doesn't need or want the safety net of a salary." I find this thinking somewhat attractive because I recognize that real achievers know their own worth and want to work within a system where there are no salary ceilings, as there often are when a certain "minimum stipend" is guaranteed to all salespeople. Under a straight-commission plan, we are free to "write our own paychecks," as the expression goes and recognize that the only thing that is going to produce results in our paychecks is our own productivity.

There are certain problems with a straight-commission plan in a telephone selling atmosphere. We need to be vitally concerned that our salespeople stay within certain boundaries in the representations they make to clients and prospects. When people are on a commission-only plan, they may be more inclined to "do anything" to get the sale; especially if they are inexperienced in selling, as are many telemarketing employees. They may, as a consequence, use too much pressure and incur the risk of alienating the business community, which none of us can afford. Moreover, because it takes a little time for the new employee to get up to speed with the task, you may not want to ask him or her to subsidize their own training in this fashion.

I have found that it is helpful to show people that they are making a living right away when they get on the phone, and if this means rewarding them for a little nonachievement, I am willing to take the risk that this behavior will not become habitual. *I suggest a combined salary and commission plan that is weighted toward the result you hope to produce—good, strong sales.* By giving the employee a symbolic guarantee, yet a very hefty commission for performance, we tend to get what we're after more times than not. Here's how it works.

Let's say you are hiring part-timers for the purpose of setting up appointments for salespeople to follow up and close. One very successful formula is to pay them

1. the *prevailing minimum wage* as a base salary, which they are entitled to whether they produce or not;
2. a *per-lead bonus* for each lead that they write and which results in an actual appointment for the salesperson; and

3. a *commission* that is based upon the number of actual closed sales that are produced as a result of the leads that were written by the telemarketing rep.

In adding up figures, we arrive at the following pay, assuming that 1) a rep writes two appointments per hour that result in 85 percent completed or verified appointments; 2) she writes two appointments on the average per hour over a twenty-hour work week, and one half of the appointments ultimately resulted in sales; and 3) we give her fifty cents for each verified appointment and two dollars for each completed sale. Here are the week's statistics:

Gross hours worked: 20 @ $3.50 per hour   = $70.00

Per-lead bonus: 40 leads written x 85% =
34 verified leads paid @ 50¢ each   = $17.00

Commissions paid on final sales:
34 leads resulted in 17 sales paid @ $2.00 apiece   = $34.00

Total pay for the week: $121.00

This formula may, of course, be adjusted in terms of the value that is given to each category of performance. For instance, the *per-lead bonus* may be reduced while the *commission* from ultimate sales is increased. This would tend to tell the rep that management is serious about the need to write leads that are solid, that result in sales. Another approach is to increase the *base wage*, but this does not have a real bearing upon performance, unless minimum production standards or quotas are announced and enforced. A *graduated bonus pay scale* may be introduced that rewards higher hourly performance along with higher percentages of closed sales from appointments written. For example, if a person produces a weekly average *LPH* or *Lead Per Hour* rate of 2.0 leads per hour, he or she will be paid at the rate of 50¢ per lead, as long as the cancellation rate does not exceed 10 percent of all leads written. If, on the other hand, the rep writes at a level of 2.5 leads per hour, he or she will receive 75¢ per lead, and if the performance reaches 3.0 leads per hour, the reward becomes $1 per lead. Thus, we are rewarding *disproportionately well* for the behavior we want to produce. In this case it is a high number of leads written.

At the same time, we may implement a graduated commission plan for percentages of leads closed by salesmen in the field. At 50 percent the telemarketing rep receives $2; at 75 percent she receives $3; and at 85 percent, she is paid $4; assuming a minimum of two leads per hour are written, thus qualifying her to participate in the graduated incentive plan.

Let's examine the pay received by three hypothetical reps under this revised plan.

	Gross Leads	Verified	LPH Average	% of Sales Closed
REP NO. 1	40	37	1.85 Hr.	60%
		$18.50		$44.40 (22.2 Sales)
REP NO. 2	55	50	2.50 Hr.	75%
		$37.50		$112.50 (37.5 Sales)
REP NO. 3	70	64	3.20 Hr.	85%
		$64.00		$217.60 (54.4 Sales)

Assuming each of the three reps receives his or her base pay of $70 for 20 hours worked, the gross pay by the end of the week for each rep is 1) Rep #1: $132.90, or $6.65 per hour; 2) Rep #2: $220.00, or $11.00 per hour; and 3) Rep #3: $351.60, or $17.58 per hour. Although Rep #3 is making almost three times what Rep #1 is making, #3 is costing your company only $6.46 for each sale he or she is contributing to, while #1 is costing $5.99 per sale produced. *In other words, it is costing the company only 7 percent more to reward the high producer in this fashion.* It is easy for any entering sales rep to see that the money is earned by those who produce a large number of leads per hour and close at a high rate. Thus, management's objective is in line with the intention of each rep to make as much money as he or she can.

Management may easily see who is producing at acceptable levels by looking at a number of indexes. For example, by inquiring about the LPH average of a given rep, management can determine whether the person is producing at a high enough hourly level to justify continuing employment. Another index is the proportion of guaranteed base pay to overall salary for a given week. In our example above, Rep #1 was receiving 52.67 percent of his salary for the week in the form of guaranteed pay. ($70.00 of the $132.90 was base pay.) Rep #2 received only 31.81 percent of salary as guaranteed pay, while Rep #3 got even less, or 19.90 percent as base pay. A "danger level" can be established at, say 60 percent, where the telemarketing supervisor is alerted that the house is supporting a rep with low production and that corrective action is needed.

All reps should know the expectations of management as to production levels. I have found that posting production figures along with salary figures, week by week, can be a very effective inducement to perform, as well as an accurate method for helping reps to see where they stand among their peers. Management may also establish group performance norms which tie into overall company performance targets. In this way, telemarketing reps can feel that they are a part of a larger team effort, and appreciate their significance in the greater functioning of the company.

To encourage peak production, management needs to make a commitment to training reps in the most effective and financially prudent manner. This may be the most significant telemarketing management variable.

HOW TO TRAIN AND RETRAIN
YOUR TELEPHONE SALES REPS

Some people simply can't hack a telephone sales job. It is a fact of life. What we need to do as telemarketing directors is discover a low-cost method of avoiding these people, if possible, and short of this, weeding them out of the company as quickly and painlessly as possible. Here are some basic tips for putting together a winning training program:

1. Screen potential TSRs (Telephone Sales Reps) by phone before consenting to a face-to-face meeting with them. Listen to their voices. Are they confident or shaky? Do they sound smooth and grammatical, or are they too unpolished? How do they respond to questions? Are they quick on the uptake, or do they sound like dummies? Why do they want this job? How much or little money do they want to make? Have they ever sold anything by phone before? What do they think it takes to be successful in selling by phone?

In short, if they pass your telephonic probing, consent to a live interview. If they have sold anything by phone before, ask them to pitch you on the phone. Even if they don't sound like good prospects, you will be learning other people's scripting strategies in this way.

2. When you interview potential reps, ask them to read your script out loud a few times. This will give you an opportunity to hear them as they will sound to prospective clients. If their reading is poor, don't hire them. Ask candidates if they will have any problem reading the script with vigor about fifty to seventy-five times per shift. If they holler, let 'em go.

3. Spend as little time in formal training as possible. The more it seems that telephone selling is difficult, the more trainees will build up resistance to the activity. The ideal amount of training time before the rep makes some calls is probably no more than 2-3 hours.

I suggest you give them some background on the company and its general goals, and then tell them what they need to accomplish to be successful. Have all calling materials prepared, including scripts, comebacks to objections, transition phrases, product knowledge capsules, and the like.

After the trainees have become familiar with these tools, role-play with them to show how actual conversations do and should sound. Be supportive. They won't be wizards right away, unless they are professionally trained in sight reading, as some actors are.

4. It is often helpful to have them pull up a chair next to a seasoned veteran in the sales room. This will give them proof that the system works. They will also receive an image of the goal for which they should strive in perfecting their performance. After they have listened for a half-hour to an hour, call them back into the training room to see if they have any questions.

5. Be prepared to let them falter in the beginning of their calling activity, but be nearby, or appoint a "buddy" for this purpose. Before the shift ends, ask your trainee how he or she did, and offer any explanations. If the rep got an order during the first shift, it can be a good sign of future performance. Make a big deal about this achievement in front of the seasoned staff. Be visible in your praise. This will make the person feel like she has earned a spot on the team. If, on the other hand, your trainee does not manage to get an order during the remainder of the first shift, be encouraging and point to tomorrow.

6. If, on the next day, the trainee still does not perform well in the early going, check to assure she is staying with the letter of the script.

Chances are very strong that she isn't, which is accounting for weak performance. You may wish to listen in on a conversation or two on your extension phone, to make sure that her attitude is positive, and she is following directions. Take notes on what you are hearing in order to offer strong feedback for improvement.

I have worked out a rule of thumb in most circumstances: if a trainee fails to make a sale within the first five hours of calling time, and you have done everything you should do in terms of training and supervision, then consider terminating the person. Chances are he will not improve significantly over the next ten, twenty, or even eighty hours in such a dramatic fashion as to make the investment of time and money worthwhile.

This may sound callous to some, but it is necessary to the proper functioning of your telemarketing section. It only serves to diminish the motivation of the winners to see a hopeless loser continue to be subsidized by management. It also shows that the supervisor is weak in her analysis of the value of the trainee if she fails to make a firm and accurate decision in a timely way. After a while, the veterans ask themselves why they are working so hard when they can just get by without threat of termination.

I have worked with some companies that resemble the civil service more than free enterprise institutions. Their motto could be: "Once hired— never fired." They will bring a recruit on board who is ill-equipped to do a job, and then keep the person in the job or transfer him to some other section where he is no more likely to succeed. This sort of foolish, costly, and professionally gutless behavior has no part in a successful telemarketing situation.

There is simply more turnover in a telemarketing environment than in a clerical department, for instance. We need to plan for it, and be prepared to *cause* the turnover ourselves to get the kind of staff we need to do the job right.

What happens when your trainee does make it past the five hour barrier? What's next? You will find that your new reps make several mistakes that require correction. First, and most important, they will deviate from the written presentation. They will introduce "weasel words" where they don't belong, even if you have trained them to avoid them. You will hear the word "like" being used, and the reps will probably start to sound soft and timid as they reach the closing portion of their presentations.

They will also rush off the phone before confirming the order. And, most significantly, they will be failing to answer objections or to attempt added closings. All of these behaviors will contribute to fewer sales than you want from the trainees.

This is why it is imperative that you spend time with each rep in *retraining*. I suggest the first retraining period be scheduled after about seven telephone hours have been logged. Your reps will have gotten their first orders and will be eager for more sophisticated ways of selling. Drill them in the basics of the presentation, while pointing out any deviations that you have noticed. Then assure them that they will do better and better if they simply stick with the formula.

The second training program should be scheduled after the rep has been on the phone about twenty hours, or at the beginning of the second week. I suggest that tape recordings be used whenever possible to let the rep hear how he actually sounds during conversations. He will be able to point out his own strengths and weaknesses, and you will be able to start and stop the tape to suggest opportune responses or strategies that might have been undertaken by the rep. This feedback should be given on a one-on-one basis in the beginning of a rep's tenure on the job. After you have a rather solid crew of seasoned people, you can play taped calls to the entire group as a way of pointing out lessons of value for everyone.

I am told that tape recording, to be in keeping with the letter of the law, should be done under one of two conditions: (1) Ask the other party if she minds if you tape record the call, before doing so; or (2) Use a phone with a beep-tone that is audible in the background of the call, emitting a tone every fifteen seconds. This will alert the caller that the call may be taped.

A major utility company in California does neither of these things, yet is still taping calls with impunity, I am informed. They commonly tape calls in the customer service department "for training purposes only," and have placed stickers on the in-house telephones announcing this fact. Apparently, the Public Utilities Commission has held that this is okay, and that notice need not be given to customers about the taping.

Most companies elect to tape calls, and simply don't bother to tell anyone outside of the firm. While technically illegal, this is the least obtrusive way of assuring quality control, it seems. As long as the tapes are not used against your customers in any way, and are expunged or erased immediately after they have served their training purpose, there is probably little harm in this method.

No matter what method you use, tape recording can provide the most accurate feedback to reps on what they are doing on the phone. Coupled with the expert evaluation and interpretation of the supervisor, this training device can result in a significant improvement within a short period of time.

WATCH OUT FOR COMPLACENCY AND YOUR "OLD PRO'S"

People do tend to rise to a level of incompetence, and indeed, they are comfortable staying there, unless prodded to do otherwise. This kind of mediocre outcome may be observed in a number of mature telephone selling situations, where certain old pros predominate. They have reached a given comfort level of productivity, from which they refuse to move upward.

Veterans can make it difficult on management because they set a production standard that new trainees try to emulate and think that they cannot exceed. If they do better than the old pros, they will be considered "rate-busters," as some people were called early in the twentieth century. As a result, they will be quietly or explicitly castigated by their fellows, with whom they wish to get along, of course.

I remember that I faced this kind of situation when I took over the management of a telephone sales room a number of years ago. There was a veteran named Ted who ruled the roost, so to speak. Whenever I would hire and train people to add to the crew, they would never outsell Ted, although I considered them capable of doing this. Finally, I decided that old Ted was inhibiting the performance of my new people. I called him into my office and informed him that I expected more sales from him, as he was not performing up to his potential. He apparently did not get the message. I finally fired him, explaining to my boss, who was shocked at the move, what my motive was in taking this action. I will never forget the thinly veiled threat contained in my boss's words to me: "I hope you're right."

I was right. After Ted's departure, I trained many new people and increased the expectations for production. Many of my people far exceeded the level that Ted had established. It is a good idea to periodically review our perceptions as to what levels of performance are appropriate for our sales crew and challenge ourselves and our people to do even better.

HOW TO BOOST SALES

I am a strong believer in the power and usefulness of frequent sales meetings. Through meetings we can cement commitment to group and individual performance objectives, while discovering any obstacles that our people confront. We can explore new selling methods and point out current market opportunities, as well.

I have found a brief meeting for about five minutes before a workshift to be a helpful exercise. During these meetings I'll discuss changes in procedure as well as tell a story or two in order to "psych up the troops." In all seriousness, life proceeds better when the supervisor does a little cheerleading. People feel better about themselves and their jobs, and also get the clear message that management cares about their achievements.

I also suggest *contests*. People love prizes, as their attendance at carnivals and game shows attests. Contests can be tremendous motivators, whether the winner wins a trip to Hawaii, a day off, or even an instant camera. Sometimes there is greater competition for the gift as its extrinsic value *decreases*, believe it or not. A number of companies have plaques that read, "Best Salesperson of the Month," or quarter, or year, that are displayed prominently at work. People who achieve such distinctions are given continuing *recognition* for their accomplishments, which is a great motivator.

Money also works! Crass though it may sound, I have been known to take currency out of my pocket and pin it on a corkboard in the front of a room, while announcing that the next "ten sales will win the cash!" This causes quite a fever-pitch of activity.

Some folks contend that we shouldn't *have* to motivate our reps with such inducements. They should simply do their best in all circumstances. I agree. Nonetheless, by adding to the sweetness of the reward, we are more likely to get what we want.

Companies have been finding out of late that including workers in decisions tends to seal their commitment to achieving certain goals. Also known as participative decision making, or *PDM*, this technique can be very helpful in a telemarketing environment. *Ask the telemarketing reps what they recommend be done to increase productivity.* Do this in and out of sales meetings, and give recognition to the most useful ideas. This will instill pride and a sense of ownership in the staff.

MANAGERS AND SUPERVISORS NEED HELP TOO!

I recognize that it is self-serving to recommend you attend telemarketing seminars from time to time, as I host a good number of these myself, yet I am convinced you will feel renewed in your purpose and resolve as a result. There is nothing quite like being surrounded by fellow professionals who are eager to share their triumphs and tragedies for your benefit and theirs. The continuing education habit is an excellent one to acquire because you will find yourself and your staff being challenged constantly to determine whether your operation could be modified in one way or another.

I know some folks think they are perfect—their businesses are expanding and they are leaders in their industries. Nonetheless, it is even more important to find tools to help you grow and stay on top of the heap. This reminds me of a line that I read in an interview with Frederick C. Crawford, the man who built Thompson Products into the giant, TRW. He points out that "a businessman should always remember that someone, somewhere, is making a product that will make his product obsolete. Always assume that there is a disaster around the corner."[1] I try to put the spirit of this idea into practice in my own business by attending seminars put on by colleagues in telemarketing and training. I find the programs reinforcing and disturbing at the same time. I am pleased to see that good ideas still occupy a place in the architecture of success, and I also hear ideas that I have either passed over in the past or have been unfamiliar with. Exposure to these notions makes me more resourceful and valuable to my clients.

[1]Frederick C. Crawford, "Ten Things I Have Learned About Management," *Mainliner*, May 1981, p. 148.

ABSENTEE SUPERVISORS NEED NOT APPLY

As you may have extrapolated from this chapter, it is very important to play a meaningful and *visible* role in the everyday operation of a telemarketing function. There are several reasons you should be "eyeballing" your sales reps during most of the working day:

1. They need your guidance. If you leave decisions about policy and procedure to the sales reps, you may be in for some surprises in the representations they make on your behalf to customers.
2. Mood swings occur quickly in telephone marketing offices. It is amazing how enthusiasm is kinetic and it energizes everybody in close proximity, and the same sort of process applies to negativity or depression. Sometimes it is important to be nearby to patrol the sales area and to psych up the troops with a word or two of encouragement.
3. To get things moving, it is helpful to show your people how easy and fun selling by phone can be. *Get on the phone, yourself, for fifteen minutes or half an hour!* Your adrenalin will probably help you to get at least a few orders, and this sight will encourage everybody else.
4. In being close by, you can confirm or disapprove the wisdom of making various personnel decisions, and you can spot key reps that may be headed for a sales slump and help them to avoid a prolonged one.
5. Your physical commitment to being on hand will encourage reps to take their role seriously as well. To test the impact of being there, I suggest you plan to disappear for specific periods of time over a few days. Note the average hourly production figures when you are there and when you are away. I guarantee that the figures will fall with your absence from the area.

HANDLING SALES REP
BURNOUT SYNDROME

You already know that selling by telephone can be grueling. Some reps who are very capable over the short term are poor finishers in the marathon that is presented by the rigors of daily telephone selling. What can we do when we think we are going to lose one of our better reps to exhaustion or apathy?

One of the first things to do is to recognize the symptoms of sales rep burnout:

1. They are absent more often. High producers are usually rather punctual and are not prone to missing work shifts.
2. They lose their competitiveness. Rather than being excited about contests and special incentives, they lie back and seem bored with the whole thing.
3. They fail to offer help to new trainees. Instead, they send them to somebody else on the crew or to management with any questtions.
4. They either grow hostile toward customers or take on an uncaring attitude toward them. They may take to slamming the telephone back into the cradle after turndowns, which should be strictly prohibited in all sales centers.
5. They grow "cold" on the product, and may share their misgivings about its desirability in public with other reps or with clients over the phone.
6. When given criticism or suggestions, they fail to offer clear feedback as to whether the items were noted and understood.
7. They may begin to question the authority or goodwill of management, while citing illustrations of better conditions elsewhere.
8. They may ask for a different assignment without heavy selling responsibilities.
9. They may sabotage their sales by failing to close orders or by selling impossibly large or unusual packages.
10. They may come to you directly, ask for your advise about a sales slump, but refuse to implement any changes offered. What they are really doing is asking you to make the career decision for them that relieves them from having to sell.

What should you do if you spot any number of these behaviors in your successful sales reps? I think there are several things that you may do to turn the situation around. First, you might recognize that the sales rep is really responding to *boredom*, more than anything else. Things have gotten too predictable for the person. This reminds me of the time I delivered an in-house training program for a company which had previously sent a sales rep to one of my public seminars for the purpose of evaluation. He apparently liked what he learned, and when I was later finishing my in-house course at his firm, I made it a point to discover how he was doing with the techniques he received. He said, with a rather downcast voice, "I guess I'm doing okay. My ratio of appointments gotten from calls made has jumped from about 20 percent to about 80 percent." I thought this was terrific, but I asked, "Why the long face, then?" He replied, "Well, it's just kinda boring, I guess, to be getting so many positive responses!"

Sometimes, as we noted in a prior chapter, salespeople have a fear of success that prevents them from being comfortable with achievement or really substantial sales growth. We need to remind them of their primary purpose in making sales and also be prepared to *resell* them on the benefits they derive from the job and are delivering to grateful clients.

Sometimes the alienated or disaffected rep needs a little recognition for his or her continuing efforts on behalf of the firm. Staging periodic awards ceremonies to honor veteran telemarketers works well, especially in concert with bestowing upon them symbols of their achievement in the form of plaques, engraved "gold" pens, mini-trips, and even comedic notions from joke shops. You might go to a local trophy store to investigate offbeat yet sensible gifts for your crew. Why not come up with a premium catalog from an advertising specialty house and encourage your reps to "go shopping" within certain price ranges or gift categories? If you run out of ideas, incorporate their suggestions as to appropriate rewards. I assure you they will come up with rewards you never thought of before!

It is also a good idea to ask a rep who is turning "cold" on the job if there is anything bothering them that they would like to share with you, either in the privacy of your office or on neutral ground such as a restaurant over coffee. Getting away from the office may open up communication channels between you that would remain closed otherwise.

If a rep is having severe psychological problems caused by drinking, drugs, or marital or intimate problems, you may wish to explore the idea of retaining a psychological counselor to help. I would suggest counseling be made available to the entire staff as a part of the benefits of the job, and they be given access to services either for the purpose of handling particular problems, or for the purpose of exploring their own psychological growth. I noted recently that one of my corporate clients, which happens to be an industry leader, offers such a program to all employees and has initiated a campaign to alert employees to its existence. Posters that explain the kinds of services that are accessible are visible in various congregation areas of the plant, near the personnel office, and in the lunchroom facility.

Circulate letters from satisfied customers to your salespeople. This will give them a real boost, as they will be reminded that their products and services are well regarded and that the purpose they serve is meaningful.

MAKE YOUR CREW FEEL SPECIAL

When I was in management with Time/Life Libraries, Inc., I had the good fortune to have worked with some very capable people from diverse backgrounds. I remember we were having a Christmas party, and one of my top producing sales reps said something to me that I have never forgotten. "Gary," he said, "I know I could make more money working somewhere else, but the reason I stay with Time/Life is because you make coming to work special. I never know what to expect next, especially from your daily sales meetings. It's better than watching Johnny Carson!"

I believe the best management philosophy isn't Theory X, or Theory Y, or even Theory Z, but Theory "Me" and Theory "You." By becoming the most genuine, imaginative, and creative managers and supervisors, I believe you will find that people who work with you respond in kind. Literally strive to be the kind of manager that you would like to work for, and you will probably get along famously with your reps, who will work their hearts out for you.

Remember something else, too. Telephone marketing is one of the most challenging and taxing methods around of doing business. In achieving success, you and your staff have something to be proud of and which relatively few people can claim as their area of expertise.

Now, reach out and *sell* someone! [TM]

Afterword

In the beginning of this book I mentioned that it is difficult to create a sense of dialogue through the typical author-to-reader exchange. You can't really ask questions as they occur to you, nor can you share illustrations and experiences that could further illuminate the ideas being presented. From this point forward, you will be trying to come to grips with the ideas shared in these pages, and I would like to have an opportunity to hear of your successes and your challenges. In fact, this is one of the main ways that I grow as an author, consultant, and speaker, so I invite you to contact me at the address below with your questions, comments, and suggestions.

If you would like to hear of forthcoming seminars in such areas as telephone effectiveness, marketing, and management, or you would like to learn more about our other publications, audio/videotapes, and newsletter, please let me know.

In the meantime, I wish you the very best.

Gary S. Goodman, Ph.D.
President,
Goodman Communications Corporation
P.O. Box 9733
Glendale, California 91206
(213) 243-7338

Index

NOW ... Announcing these other fine books from Prentice-Hall—

WINNING BY TELEPHONE: Telephone Effectiveness for Business Professionals and Consumers, by Gary S. Goodman. Emphasizing business communications, this book offers proven techniques for improving telephone effectiveness based on the author's experience as a communication consultant and a Telephone Effectiveness Seminar leader. In addition to a special chapter devoted to helping consumers "Fight Back By Telephone," it includes chapters on how to control conversations, gather information, listen more effectively, reduce telephone stress, and speak with authority and influence.

$5.95 paperback, $14.95 hardcover

SUCCESSFUL SELLING FROM A TO $: The Professional's Guide to Money-Making Strategies, by John W. Rice. Ideal for both salespeople and sales managers, this book presents scores of money-making techniques that have been used successfully by the author over the past 35 years. Emphasizing a professional approach, it covers virtually every subject for which selling demands expertise, presenting several aspects in new light and new detail. Discusses analysis of needs, buyer motives, sales presentations, objectives, allocation of time, distributor organizations, and closing techniques.

$6.95 paperback, $12.95 hardcover

To order these books, just complete the convenient order form below and mail to Prentice-Hall, Inc., General Publishing Division, Attn. Addison Tredd, Englewood Cliffs, N.J. 07632

Title	Author	Price*

Subtotal _____

Sales Tax (where applicable) _____

Postage & Handling (75¢/book) _____

Total $ _____

Please send me the books listed above. Enclosed is my check ☐ Money order ☐ or, charge my VISA ☐ MasterCard ☐ Account # _____

Credit card expiration date _____

Name _____

Address _____

City _____ State _____ Zip _____

Prices subject to change without notice. Please allow 4 weeks for delivery.